MARINA TSVETAEVA
THE ESSENTIAL POETRY

Glagoslav Publications

MARINA TSVETAEVA
THE ESSENTIAL POETRY

Translated by
Michael M. Naydan and **Slava I. Yastremski**

With a Translator's Introduction and
With a special poet's Guest Introduction by **Tess Gallagher**

Book created by Max Mendor

© 2015, Glagoslav, Nederland

Glagoslav Publications Ltd
88-90 Hatton Garden
EC1N 8PN London
United Kingdom

www.glagoslav.com

ISBN: 978-17-84379-58-2

This book is in copyright. No part of this publication may be reproduced, stored in a retrieval system or transmitted in any form or by any means without the prior permission in writing of the publisher, nor be otherwise circulated in any form of binding or cover other than that in which it is published without a similar condition, including this condition, being imposed on the subsequent purchaser.

Contents

ACKNOWLEDGMENTS 7
TRANSLATING THE FINE EXCESS OF SPIRIT IN MARINA TSVETAEVA 9
THE SEVEN SNAKESKINS OF MARINA TSVETAEVA'S POETRY 15
FROM EVENING ALBUM (1910) 21
FROM MAGIC LANTERN (1912) 27
FROM POEMS OF ADOLESCENCE (1913-1915) 31
FROM MILEPOSTS I (1916) 39
FROM POEMS FOR BLOK (1922) 49
FROM THE SWAN'S ENCAMPMENT (1917-1920) 55
FROM MILEPOSTS II (1922) 59
FROM CRAFT (1923) 65
FROM AFTER RUSSIA (1928) 71
FROM POEMS NOT PUBLISHED IN COLLECTIONS 95
POEM OF THE MOUNTAIN (1924) 105
POEM OF THE END (1924) 117
ENDNOTES 149
A NOTE ON THE TRANSLATORS 161

*This translation is dedicated to Carol Ueland,
a fellow traveler along the poetry road
and a great friend and colleague over the years.*

Acknowledgments

"There is an hour for those words..." first appeared in *Confrontation* No. 48-49 (Spring/Summer 1992). The following translations appeared initially in Marina Tsvetaeva *After Russia* Trans. Michael M. Naydan with Slava Yastremski (Ann Arbor: Ardis Publishers, 1992): "Nocturnal whispers: a hand...," "The Balcony," "Someone rides to mortal victory...," "With what inspiration...," "There are ashes of treasures...," "Ophelia to Hamlet," "Ophelia in Defense of the Queen," "Wires," "In Praise of Time," "Dialogue of Hamlet with his Conscience," "A Minute," "The Prague Knight," "Nocturnal Places," "An Attempt at Jealousy," and "A yataghan? A fire?...." Most of the translations published in the *After Russia* collection have been revised for this edition.

Extra special thanks to Tess Gallagher for her insightful suggestions on the final version of this manuscript that have served to fine tune these translations and also for her kindness in providing her poet's guest introduction to the volume.

Our special gratitude to Max Mendor for his patience and all his meticulous efforts in designing this volume.

Translating the fine excess of spirit in Marina Tsvetaeva

Marina Tsvetaeva holds a very special place in my memory of the search for women writers who might offer examples of what to admire and to which we might aspire.

The early 1970s female models for young women poets like myself, as we began to form our poetic voices, were either hermetic such as Emily Dickinson—who was shuttered away, with her bounty hidden in mason jars because her genius had been thwarted by male publishing predilections—or at the other end of the scale, the explosive cauldron of pent up righteous anger and truth-telling of Sylvia Plath and Ann Sexton—for which one was grateful, while feeling guiltily that one had perhaps been ritually saved by their suicides from similar psychic trauma.

When translations by Stanley Kunitz and others of Tsvetaeva's contemporary luminary Anna Akmatova began to be published, I consequently felt myself drinking deeply of the latter's gravitas, a kind of dignity and regal purity, a seemingly uncrushable spirit, a poet who, while representing the weight of oppression of those times under Stalin, had managed to become a fortress unto herself, yet who would come to embody that time.

But Marina Tsvetaeva was another equally powerful and compelling voice emerging from Russia. I truly believe that Kunitz (an excellent translator of Akhmatova and, who eventually became my mentor after I wrote thanking him for those poems) was really thinking of Tsvetaeva's influence on me when he referred to my work as possessing a "fine excess of spirit." Akhmatova held her truths close to the bone so we were able to suck the marrow of those cold Russian realities, but Tsvetaeva's spirit could not articulate or survive without soaring.

In my early readings of Tsvetaeva it is precisely this excess, this sense that life is at once abundant and dire that attracted me, and further, that at life's bleakest moments, one might be lifted by love and language into something surpassing the merely mortal. These new rangier, emotionally freighted translations of Tsvetaeva by Michael Naydan and Slava Yastremski, the latter a native Russian speaker and professor at Bucknell University, and the former a professor and translator at Penn State University, who have translated Russian prose and poetry for the past forty years, make these qualities much more strongly available to me. Across the translations of Akhmatova there still remains only one Akhmatova for me. But with Tsvetaeva there exist many Tsvetaevas, and these further inflections are worth discovering in this considerable accomplishment.

The truth of this multiplicity of Tsvetaevas was brought strongly home to me when I was fortunate enough to attend a marvelous program presented in Dublin of Tsvetaeva's work translated into Irish. The translator herself, Dairena Ní Chinnéide, gave an unforgettable voicing of these poems, against the excellent English translations read commandingly by their creator Elaine Feinstein. Next to the English emerged this Irish spitfire Tsvetaeva, who was guttural and utterly tenacious, imperious even. Her language in Irish, a spiritual spiraling to a pinnacle, carried us into the vastness of Tvetaeva's imagination, which is always a feeling of going toward something as much as it is a rendering of what one could actually possess.

These translations offered by Naydan and Yastremski seem to closely accompany the Tsvetaeva who really wants to love like the gods, not like a mere human being. She changes the entire scale of our expectation of how one loves and whom one loves. For her personally, this became a recipe for loss since it was not easy to find lovers who could soar with her. And of course those heights could not be maintained, even when she chose poets as love mates whether actualized (such as her early female lover Sophia Parnok) or kindred in spirit (Blok, Rilke, Akhmatova) or somewhere in between (Mandelstam and Pasternak).

What I became more aware of while reading these translations is how Tsvetaeva uses her poetry to regain her emotional balance. Instead of cutting a lover off for leaving her, or becoming the victim, she turns the tables on them and lets them feel what *they* have lost in abandoning *their* love of her. This was a newly articulated paradigm for women poets all over the world trying to do more than lick wounds in the stance of a victim.

In placing Tsvetaeva's appeal to American contemporary poetry of the present and myself in the 1970s, I believe she has been the more dangerous and unwieldy model when compared to Akhmatova, who became so important to us as a sign of stature under political and emotional duress, attracting translators such as Jane Kenyon whose own work was greatly emboldened by Akhmatova. For all the possible range of voices open to women poets, what still claims central respect in the American canon and critical arena, truncated as that apparatus may be, seems fairly "reeled in"—selves in chiarascuro—emotional cargoes held close to the chest. We seem to have a kind of "cool hand Luke" censor built into both female and male engendered poetry—but especially operative toward poetry written by women.

When one reads Tsvetaeva in Naydan and Yastremksi's translations, I find something restored to her that I had deeply sensed, yet could not quite experience: a rough grasping toward language that is willing for the inelegant if it serves the passion of her impulse in the moment. Also present here is the Tsvetaeva who lets—rather who *encourages*—the poem to carry her off on its wild galloping back. The wonder is how she revisits the enigma of her life situations in the poems and extends this wildness, line-by-line, verse-by-verse, bringing that untamed quality forward as a virtue.

How much we would have lost had Tsvetaeva not formed this incremental way of working backward and forward at the same time. This process, visible to me in these translations, certified and extended her power as we follow her, reassessing and adding like box cars, the next installment of her emotional but galvanized offering.

Unlike what I sense about Akhmatova, I never feel Tsvetaeva towering apart from me. She is always a woman loving like a woman—heedless and remorselessly, full of savoring and overreach, but haughty too and in the plenitude of her beauty, both physical and spiritual. Because of that very face-to-face quality, that open admission of love, given in a holy register, yet human too in its loss and sorrow, we all the more accompany her. There is something swashbuckling and Joan of Arcish, something dashing in her when one has more of the punctuation as she used it given in this translation. The plenitude of dashes and exclamations are important musical scorings for her and rendered closely here.

Perhaps one can say these translations excel in not being too smoothed out with housekeeping that could subdue the spirit in Tsvetaeva's case. We need both kinds of translations, of course, those that let a writer wear fully the stature of the English she might have given us, had she written in English, but also a translation, such as this one, which allows us the sometimes ragged and see-through of English as a cracked vessel, which can't quite carry, but miraculously *does* carry—this most venturing, most high stakes Russian spender of the heart's meaty core—Marina Tsvetaeva.

Tess Gallagher
Bay Street, Pt. Angeles, Washington
August 2014

The seven snakeskins of Marina Tsvetaeva's poetry

Marina Tsvetaeva's poetry is at times not easy to comprehend in the original Russian, much less in translation. A terse, elliptical style with myriad dashes and exclamation points characterizes much of her mature verse, as does a verbal playfulness that has multiple layers of meaning both direct and implied or echoed. Her poems often contain auditory rebuses that require some effort to solve. Readers solve them by filling in the gaps left by ellipses. We as translators must do the same. Other poetic features that Tsvetaeva's readers encounter include, for example, colloquialisms that she puts into conversation with Old Church Slavonicisms, fusing elements of the past and a lofty style with her colloquial present, all done in an innovative way. As Tsvetaeva herself has indicated, she was happy for the "miracle of understanding" of just a single reader. That "miracle of understanding" over time has increased exponentially as more and more readers have taken the time to delve more deeply into her poetry. The reader's task of decoding her may be difficult, but, nevertheless, highly rewarding.

Tsvetaeva herself has written about the "seven snake skins" of her poetic personae and, by implication, a complex variety of styles that has developed over time. Her poetry has changed markedly over the course of her creative lifespan from collection to collection, from her unimposing juvenilia to her consistently compelling poetry that begins to blossom between 1915 and 1916. On occasion in her early poetry she does manage to create a minor masterpiece as in her outstanding poem "A Prayer," written on her birthday in 1909. To borrow her own locution from the title of one of her essays, you might say that Tsvetaeva is a "poet with a history" as opposed to one without—a poet such as Anna Akhmatova, whom Tsvetaeva notes was virtually born writing in a remarkable style that never changed over the course of her creative lifetime. Moreover, to appropriate Tsvetaeva's description of Boris Paternak's poetry as a "downpour of light," one might say that Tsvetaeva's poetry functions as a downpour of sound: the acoustic properties of her verse are best understood when read aloud. We try to imitate those acoustic elements of her poetry whenever possible in the translations, or present it at times in a compensatory way.

Tsvetaeva's life, to which she alludes continually in her poetry, was a tragic one. She lost her mother at an early age, her child Irina to starvation, her homeland through emigration to Europe in 1922 after the Russian Civil War, numerous loves including the poet Sophia Parnok and the former White Army officer Konstantin Rodzevich; her husband, who was executed by the Bolsheviks; and, eventually, her own life—to suicide in 1941 after she had returned to the USSR two years earlier to follow her husband to his and her own impending doom in a final courageous act of duty. Yet Tsvetaeva transcended tragedy by using it to animate her poetic imagination. Her losses served as a constant source of creativity for her. To borrow a phrase from an interview the bard Leonard Cohen once gave in response to a question about his muse, I would call one of Tsvetaeva's sources of inspiration the muse of psychic catastrophe. For her readers, Tsvetaeva bares her soul and most intimate emotional experiences. That means she shares both her ecstasy as well as her despair.

Love was essential for Tsvetaeva's sense of being. Her notion of love, though, never seemed to quite fit her reality and those with whom she came into intimate personal contact. In a letter, she once described herself as lava (*lavina*) in the way she overwhelms the object of her affection. She also loved people such as the poets Anna Akhmatova and Boris Pasternak from afar, *in absentia* (*zaochno*), but with extraordinary intensity. Manic moments when she was completely infatuated and in a transcendent realm led her to a desperate desire that those she loved love her back in the same lofty way—with their entire being. Yet the objects of her desire never materialized that kind of sustained, idealized love for her; at best their love was short-lived. For Tsvetaeva, a deep well of sadness would ensue upon crashing back down to the earthly realm to her often dismal reality.

Through poetry that is intimately and inexorably tied to her biography—poems that are often overtly or covertly addressed to or associated with a particular person—she transcended her mundane and difficult life (what she calls her *byt*). She reached spiritual transcendence and the state of elation (her *bytiyo*) she so desired. Indeed, poetry was one of her main sources of salvation. At a Tsvetaeva symposium at Yale University in 1984, I recall Joseph Brodsky, in his keynote speech, calling Tsvetaeva one of the most metaphysical of Russian poets and on par with John Donne. He also compared her to Gerard Manley Hopkins for her linguistic playfulness. I wholly agree with Brodsky's intuitive pronouncements and would add that Tsvetaeva's quest for absolute love and her striving for transcendence through the metaphysical are closely intertwined. The physical aspect of love often seemed to impede her search for love's true spiritual essence.

*

My first foray into translating Tsvetaeva comprised tackling her most complex collection – *After Russia* (1928). That translation underwent at least six redactions before it was published in 1992. It was accomplished with the enormous assistance of my long-time friend and native Russian collaborator Slava Yastremski, who is extremely knowledgeable in all things literary regarding the Russian language and culture. It was aided as well by the perspicacious suggestions of my editor at Ardis Publishers at the time—Mary Ann Szporluk, who helped to make the English versions more accessible for the Anglophone reader. I initiated drafts of that translation at the urging of my dissertation advisor John Malmstad at Columbia University in part with the hope of gaining that Tsvetaevan "miracle of understanding" for my dissertation, which focused on the omnipresent theme of time (both quotidian and sacred) in Tsvetaeva's collection. Since then I have also wanted to create a more complete picture of Tsvetaeva's numerous poetic snakeskins in translation. This book attempts to do that by translating poems from each of Tsvetaeva's published collections of lyric poetry, several poems not published in collections, as well as Tsvetaeva's two most famous dramatic long poems "Poem of the Mountain" and "Poem of the End," which comprise variations on the same theme of love lost regarding the same events and time period in Tsvetaeva's life. Tsvetaeva, too, had a penchant for writing what she called "flocks" of poems, cycles. Limitations of space do not permit the inclusion of many of the longer cycles such as "Girlfriend" and "Poems for Blok" in their entirety here.

In translating Tsvetaeva, I should say a few words about her unique use of punctuation in her poetry, particularly the dash (that divides and links words or parts of words or also serves as a natural pause) and the exclamation mark (that indicates her high level of emotionality). We do largely maintain Tsvetaeva's dashes in these translations, which promote her penchant for parallelism and invoke a visual response from the reader. In some instances, the dash indicates quoted speech or the absent "to be" verb in the present tense in Russian. The reader should be able to intuit when that is the case by the context.

We also have provided a number of footnotes in this edition. Besides an exceedingly complex poetics, Tsvetaeva has an enormous number of literary, mythological, Biblical, and personal references in her poetry. Thus those notes serve as a guide for the reader for quick reference if s/he so desires.

By nature, all translation comprises a process of interpretation. At some points we feel a necessity to fill in the gaps of Tsvetaeva's elliptical verse and present our understanding of what she means. As all great works of art, Tsvetaeva's poetry is subject to not just a single interpretation. In our translations we also attempt to present Tsvetaeva's predilection for auditory effects in her poetry by imitating or approximating her alliterations and meaningful rhymes whenever we can. That has not been possible in every case.

These translations do comprise our attempt to best approximate Tsvetaeva's high art for an Anglophone audience. She, of course, cannot help but be infinitely better and the genius that she was (and continues to be for contemporary readers) in the original Russian.

— Michael M. Naydan

From
EVENING ALBUM
(1910)

THE SUICIDE

It was an evening of music and tenderness,
Everything in the cottage garden blooming.
His mother's eye shone when
She looked into his pensive eyes!
After she had disappeared in the pond
And the circles of the water had calmed,
He realized that an evil sorcerer
Had lured her there with the wave of his evil wand.
A flute from a distant *dacha* sobbed
In the radiance of pinkish rays...
He understood — before this, he was someone's,
Now he's become a beggar who's no one's.
He cried out "Momma!" one more time,
Then made his way, as though raving,
To his small bed without a word
About his dear mother in the pond.
Though above his pillow there was an icon,
He was frightened! "Please come home!"
...He sobbed quietly. Suddenly from the balcony
A voice called to him: "My baby boy!"
....
In an elegant slender envelope they found
Her "Forgive me" note: "Love and sorrow together
Are always stronger than death."[1]
Stronger than death... Yes, they are!..

DIE STILLE STRASSE

Die stille Strasse: young leaves
Brightly rustle, bending over the fence,
At home — in a dream... With a radiant child's gaze
We look upward, where the azure grows dim.

With vacant faces we repeat the German words
In a chorus after Fräulein.
And having begun to daydream, the air is silent,
In which an evening bell can barely be heard singing.

Footsteps resound sharply in a steady beat.
Die stille Strasse has made its farewell with the day
And peacefully sleeps to the rustle of trees.

That's right. We'll still sigh time and again over
Its loss on the path, in boundless Moscow.
The street whose name remains a mystery for us.

A PRAYER

Christ and God! I thirst for a miracle
Here, right now, at the break of day!
O, let me die while all of life
Is still like a book for me.

You're wise. You will not sternly say:
"Endure, your time has not yet come."
You have given me far too much!
I thirst at once for every road!

I want it all: with a gypsy's heart
To go to pilfer to the tune of a song,
To suffer for all to the sound of an organ
To rush into battle like an Amazon;

To tell fortunes in a black tower by the stars,
To lead children onward through the shadows...
So yesterday would become a legend,
So every day would be a mad spree!

I love the cross, the silk, the helmets.
My soul is but a trail of moments...
You gave me a childhood better than a fairy tale,
Now give me death at seventeen!
                          Tarusa, September 26, 1909[2]

ANOTHER PRAYER

I once again kneel before You, Lord,
In the distance having seen Your starry crown.
Let me understand, Christ, that all is not just shadows,
Let me embrace something other than a shadow at last!

I am worn out by these long days
Without a concern, without a goal, always in a partial
                                          haze...
You can love shadows, but can you live with shadows
At the age of eighteen on the earth?

After all they sing and write that happiness is at the beginning!
I wish I could blossom with my entire rejoicing soul!
But isn't it true: there's no happiness, of course, outside of sadness?
Besides the dead, there aren't any friends, are there?

After all, have those kindled by a different faith for ages
Hidden from the world in the desertedness of deserts?
No, no need for smiles acquired at the price
Of desecrating divine sacraments.

I don't need bliss at the price of humiliation.
I don't need love! I'm not mourning over it.
Allow me, Savior, to give up my soul — only shadows
Inhabit the quiet kingdom of my beloved shades.

Moscow, Fall 1910

From
MAGIC LANTERN
(1912)

MARINA TSVETAEVA

TO MOMMA

How much dark oblivion has forever
Carried away from her heart!
We remember her sad lips and
Her sumptuous strands of hair,

A lingering sigh above a notebook
And a ring with bright rubies,
While your face smiled
Above our children's bed.

We remember your youthful sorrow
Over wounded birds
And tiny droplets of tears on your long lashes
After the piano had grown silent.

AFTER THE GUESTS LEAVE

Now they're leaving. The gate has begun to sing
In the distance in a doleful screech.
An oh so sorrowful note...
Now they're gone.

Why did momma take off her earrings?
And unlatch her bracelets,
Put away the candy in a little cupboard
As though she were locking it in prison.

Momma dresses the red furniture,
The delight of the children, in slipcovers...
This is always the way it is
After all the guests have gone!

AUTUMN IN TARUSA

The bright morning isn't hot,
You run through the meadow lightly clad.
A barge slowly slips
Down the Oka River.

You keep repeating certain words
Against your will.
Somewhere bells in the field
Are weakly jingling.

Is it in the field? Or in the meadow?
Are they on their way to thresh the grain?
Eyes glance for an instant
Into someone's fate.

The blue distance between pines,
 Chatting and humming in the threshing barn...
And autumn smiles
To our spring.

Life has flown wide open, nevertheless...
Ah, sweet golden days!
How distant they are, God!
Lord, how distant they are!

MARINA TSVETAEVA

TO LITERARY PROSECUTORS

Should I conceal everything, so people would forget,
Like melted snow and a melted candle?
Be just a handful of dust in the future
Beneath a grave's cross? I don't want that!

Every instance, trembling from pain,
I return again to just one thing:
To die forevermore! Is this why
I'm given to understand everything by fate?

The evening in the nursery, where I'll sit down
To play with my dolls, a strand of a spider's web in
                                              the meadow,
A soul condemned by the way it looks...
To live it for everyone and to understand all!

For this I (power is in the revealed)
Give up for judgment everything dear to me,
So that youth would eternally keep
My restless adolescence.

From
POEMS OF ADOLESCENCE
(1913-1915)

*

I dedicate these lines
To those who'll ready my coffin.
They'll open up my high and
Detestable brow.

Changed for no reason,
With a tiny wreath on my brow,
I'll lie in the coffin
A stranger to my own heart.

You won't notice on my face:
"I hear everything! I see all!
In the coffin it hurts even more
To be like everyone else."

In a snow-white dress — a color I've hated
Since childhood!
Will I lie down — with someone nearby? —
Till the end of time?

Listen! — I won't accept it!
This is a trap!
It's not me they'll lower into the ground,
Not me.

I know! — Everything will burn to a crisp!
And the grave will give no shelter
To anything I loved
Or by which I lived.

Moscow, Spring 1913

*

For my poems, written so early,
When I didn't even know I was — a poet,
Flitting off like splashes from a fountain,
Like rocket sparks from fireworks,

Like little demons forcing their way
Into a sanctuary, where there is sleep and incense,
For my poems about youth and death,
 — For my unread poems!

Scattered in dust in bookstores
Where no one has bought or will buy them,
For my poems, like expensive wines,
Their time will come.
Koktebel, May 13, 1913

*

With great tenderness — because
Soon I will be leaving you all —
I'm rethinking who'll
Get my wolf fur coat,

Who'll get — my body-caressing plaid
And the thin walking stick with the head of a Borzoi,
And who'll get — my silver bracelet
Speckled with turquoise...

And all my notes and all my flowers
That I can't take care of...
My last rhyme — and you,
My last night!

September 22, 1915

*

I was given both a pleasant voice
And the enchanting curve of my brow,
Fate has kissed me on the lips,
Fate has taught me to excel.

I have paid a generous tribute to lips,
I have scattered roses over coffins...
But Fate has grabbed me on the run
By the hair with its heavy hand!

December 31, 1915

GIRLFRIEND[3]

1

Are you happy? Won't You say? Hardly!
It's better — just let it be!
It seems you've kissed far too many others,
Hence my sorrow.

All the heroines of Shakespeare's tragedies
I see in You.
No one has been able to save You,
Tragic youthful lady.

You've become so tired of repeating
A lover's cantillation!
The cast-iron band on your bloodless hand —
Is so revealing!

I love You. — The way the thundercloud
Over You is — a sin —
For You being so caustic and biting
And better than all the rest,

For us and our lives being so different
In the darkness of roads,
For Your inspired temptations
And fate so dark,

For me saying good-bye to You,
My stern-browed demon,
For You — no matter what I do! —
Cannot be saved!

For this trembling, for — am I really
Dreaming a dream? —
For this ironic allure,
That You aren't — him.[4]

October 16, 1914

2

I beckon yesterday's dream
To the caress of a plush lap throw.
What was this? – Who was the victor? –
And who – the vanquished?

I'm rethinking everything again,
Tormenting myself with everything anew.
Was there love in that,
for which I don't have a word?

Who was the hunter? – And who – the trophy?
All is diabolically upside down!
What did the Siberian cat
Understand of this, purring all the time?

In this duel of self-wills
Who was just holding a ball?
Whose heart – was it Yours or mine
That raced at a gallop?

Anyway – what was this?
What do I long for and regret?
So I don't know: was I the victor?
Or the vanquished?

October 23, 1914

Remember: one hair on my head is more precious
To me than all other heads combined.
Go your way... "You, too,
And You too, and You."

Fall out of love with me, fall out of love with me, everyone!
Watch over someone other than me early in the morning!
So I can serenely step outside
And just stand in the wind.

May 6, 1915

From
MILEPOSTS I
(1916)

MARINA TSVETAEVA

I opened an iron box.
I took out a tearful gift.
A ring with an enormous pearl,
With a pearl so huge.

I snuck onto the porch like a cat,
Setting off with my face into the wind.
The wind blew, birds swarmed,
Swans to the left, to the right – ravens...
Our paths are — in different directions.

You'll leave — with the first clouds,
Your path will be through a forest deep
through burning sands.

You'll spend your soul — calling out.
You'll cry out — your eyes.

And above me — an owl will scream,
And above me — the grass will rustle.

Moscow January 1916

*

I planted a tiny apple tree:
For little ones — a toy,
For an old person — youth,
For the gardener — joy.

I lured a white turtledove
Into the bed chamber:

For the thief — an annoyance,
For the woman of the house — delight.

I gave birth to a little daughter —
A blue-eyed one,
A turtledove — by her voice,
A tiny little sun — by her hair.
To the woe of maidens,
To the woe of young men.

January 23, 1916

POEMS ABOUT MOSCOW

1

Clouds — everywhere,
Cupolas — all around.
Over all of Moscow —
As long as my hands can do it!
I raise you up, my finest burden,
My weightless
Tree!

In this wondrous city,
In this peaceful city,
Where I'd feel joyous
Even if I were dead —
For you to reign, for you to mourn,
To accept the crown,
O my first-born!

You fast during Lent,
Don't blacken your brows,
And respect all
Fortyfold churches.
Walk all over — in youthful stride! —
The entire expanse
Of the seven hills.

Your turn will come:
It will also be your daughter
To whom you'll give away your Moscow
With tender bitterness.
For me now unbroken sleep, the ringing of bells,
The early dawns
At Vagankovo Cemetery.[5]

March 31, 1916

POEMS FOR AKHMATOVA

1

O Muse of lament, the most beautiful of all the muses!
O you, wild[6] offspring of the white night![7]
You send a black snowstorm into Rus,
And your wails pierce us like arrows.

We dash and a muffled: oh! —
The hundred-thousandth — pledges to you: Anna
A(k)h-matova! This name is a colossal sigh,
And it falls into a depth that has no name.

We are crowned by the fact that we tread on
The same earth as you, that the sky above us is the same,
And whoever is mortally wounded by your fate
Already goes to her deathbed as an immortal.

The cupolas shine in my singing city,
And a wandering blind man glorifies the bright
Church of the Savior... And I give you my city of bells
As a gift, Akhmatova! — and also my heart.

June 19, 1916

*

In days of olde you were like a mother to me,
I could call you in the middle of the night,
The light of feverishness, the light of sleeplessness,
The light of my eyes in nights of olde.

Full of grace, remember,
Sunsetless days of olde,
Both a mother's and a daughter's,
Sunsetless, eveningless.

I haven't come to trouble you, but only to say good-bye,
I'll just kiss the hem of your dress,
And I'll look into your eyes with my eyes
That used to be kissed in nights of olde.

There will be a day — when I'll die — and a day — when
                                                     you will too,

There will be a day — when I understand — and a day —
                                              when you will too.
And on that day of forgiveness[8]
That irretrievable time will return to us.

                                              April 26, 1916

INSOMNIA

2

I love to kiss
Hands, and I love
To give out names,
And also — to open up
Doors!
  — Wide open — into dark night!

Clasping my head,
Listening as a heavy gait
Lightens somewhere,
As the sleepy wind
Sways the sleepless
Forest.

Ah, the night!
Somewhere springs are running,
Inclined – to sleep.
I'm almost asleep.
Somewhere in the night
Someone is drowning.

                                              May 27, 1916

3

In this huge city of mine there is — night.
From a sleepy home I go — away.
And people think: a daughter, a wife —
But I recalled just one thing: night.

July wind is sweeping the path for me,
And through the window somewhere faint music is — heard.
O, today it's for the wind to blow — till dawn
Through the thin walls of the chest — into a chest.

There is a black poplar, and in the window — light,
And a bell in a tower, and a flower — in a hand,
And that footstep following — after — no one,
And this shadow here, but I am — gone.

Lights — like threads of golden beads,
The taste of a nocturnal leaf in your — mouth.
Free yourself from daily fetters,
Friends, remember, I'm being dreamt — by you.

July 17, 1916

5

Today I am a heavenly guest
In your land.
I saw the sleeplessness of the forest
And the sleep of the fields.

Somewhere in the night horseshoes
Tore up the grass.
A cow sighed heavily
In a sleepy cowshed.

With sadness I'll tell you,
With all tenderness,
About a guard — goose
And sleeping geese.

Hands drowned in canine fur,
The dog was — gray.
Then, toward six,
It began to dawn.

July 20, 1916

6

This night I am alone in the night —
Sleepless, a homeless nun! —
This night I have the keys
To all the gates of the one and only capital city!

Insomnia pushed me on my way.
  — O, how beautiful you are to me,
                     my dimly lit Kremlin! —
This night I kiss the breast
Of the entire round warring earth!

It's not hair that stands on end — but fur,
And a stifling wind blows straight into my soul.
This night I pity everyone —
Both those being pitied and those being kissed.

August 1, 1916

7

Tenderly — tender, delicately — delicately
Something whistled in a pine tree.
I saw a child with eyes of black
In a dream.

This is the way hot resin drips
From a small red pine.
This is the way in my beautiful night
A saw blade passes through my heart.

August 8, 1916

From
POEMS FOR BLOK
(1922)

POEMS FOR BLOK[9]

1

Your name's — a bird in the hand,
Your name's — a bit of ice on the tongue.
A single-solitary movement of lips.
Your name's — four letters long.[10]
A tiny ball caught in flight,
A silver bell in the mouth.

This way a stone thrown into a placid pond,
Will sob when it sounds your name.
In the slight clicking of nocturnal hooves
Your clamorous name thunders.
And a clearly clicking rifle cock
Will say it pressed to my temple.

Your name — ah, it's forbidden! —
Your name's — a kiss to the eyes,
On the tender cold of motionless eyelids
Your name is — a kiss on the snow,
A brook's icy light blue gulp...
With your name — sleep is deep.

April 15, 1916

2

Tender specter,
A knight without reproach,
By whom are you summoned
Into my young life?

You stand in the gray —
Fog, clothed
In a snowy vestment.

It's not the wind
That chases me through the city:
Ah, it's already the third
Evening I sense the enemy.

Blue-eyed —
The snowy bard
Has bewitched me.

A snow swan
Spreads feathers at my feet.
The feathers soar
And slowly disappear in the snow.

And so, along the feathers,
I walk to the door
Beyond which is — death.

He sings to me
Beyond the deep blue windows.
He sings to me
With distant bells.

With a long shout,
With a swanlike shriek —
It calls.

Tender specter!
I know I'm dreaming all this.
Just do me one favor:
Amen, amen, disintegrate!
Amen.

May 1, 1916

3

You pass to the West of the Sun.
You'll see the evening light.
You pass to the West of the Sun,
And a snowstorm covers your tracks.

Past my windows — dispassionate —
You pass in snowy silence,
My beautiful (righteous) man of God,
Quiet light of my soul!

I do not covet your soul!
Your path is hallowed for me.
I will not hammer a nail
Into your hand, pale from kisses.

I will not summon you by name,
I will not outstretch my hands.
I will bow down from the distance
To your waxen holy face.

Standing beneath slowly falling flakes,
Into the snow I will fall on my knees,

And for your holy name
It is that evening snow I will kiss —

There, where you passed in sepulchral silence
With a majestic gait,
Silent light — holy glories —
The Almighty of my soul.

May 2, 1916

4

For the beast — a den,
For the pilgrim — a road,
For a dead man — a hearse,
To each — his own.

For a woman — to be coy.
For a tsar — to rule,
And for me — to sing the glory of
Your name.

May 2, 1916

From
THE SWAN'S ENCAMPMENT
(1917-1920)

THE RIVER DON[11]

2

He who survived — will die, he who is dead — will rise.
And here descendants, having remembered times of olde,
                                                       will say:
"Where were you?" The question crashes like thunder,
The answer crashes the same way: "On the River Don!"

"What did you do there?" "We accepted suffering,
Then grew weary and lay down to sleep."
And in the dictionary pensive grandsons
After the word "duty" will write the words: "The River
                                                       Don."

March 17, 1918

ANDRE CHENIER[12]

1

Andre Chenier ascended onto the scaffold,
Yet I live — and this is a terrible sin.
There are times — iron ones — for everyone.
And it's not a singer singing in gun powder.

And it's not a father who, trembling,
Tears away the warrior's armor from his son.
There are times when the sun is — a mortal sin.
It's not a human being — who lives in our days.

April 17, 1918

2

In the darkness I can't recognize
Hands — are they mine or someone else's?
The black conciergeries *dart about*
In a frightening dream.

Hands drop a notebook,
They grope for a thin neck.
The morning skulks like a thief.
I won't be able to finish my writing.

April 17, 1918

*

For the flesh is — flesh, for the spirit is — spirit,
For the flesh is — bread, for the spirit is — tidings,
For the flesh is — worms, for the spirit is — a sigh,
Seven crowns, seven heavens.[13]

Weep already, flesh! — Tomorrow is dust!
Spirit do not weep! — Glory to You, spirit!
Today — a slave, tomorrow — a king
For all seven — heavens.

May 9, 1918

From
MILEPOSTS II
(1922)

For Anna Akhmatova

Universal migration has begun in darkness.
It is trees wandering through — the nocturnal earth,
It is clusters of grapes fermenting — as golden wine ,
It is the stars roaming — from house to house ,
These are rivers beginning their path — backward!
And I want to lie my head on your chest and — sleep.

January 14, 1917

*

As soon as I close my burning eyelids —
Roses and rivers of paradise...

Somewhere off in the distance
As though in oblivion, —
The tender articulations
Of the serpent of paradise.

And I recognize,
Pensive Eve,
The Lord's tree
In the perfect circle of paradise.[14]

January 20, 1917

*

Dear fellow travelers, sharing a night's lodging with us!
Miles, more miles, and miles, and stale bread.

The rumbling of gypsy wagons,
The rumble of rivers running —
Backward...

Ah, at a paradisal, early, gypsy dawn —
Remember the hot neighing and the steppe all in silver?
Blue smoke on a mountain,
And a song about the king of —
The gypsies...

At black midnight, beneath the cover of ancient branches,
We have given you sons — as beautiful — as the night,
Sons — destitute — as the night...
And a nightingale trilled —
Glory...

The fellow travelers of a wondrous time failed to hold you up,
Wretched pleasures and our wretched feasts.
Campfires flamed hotly,
And onto our carpets the stars —
Fell...

January 29, 1917

*

I gazed into your eyes
Dully and with dread.
Somewhere the thunder sternly — answered.
"Oh, you're so young!
Let me tell
Your earthly lot."

Dark blue clouds swirled into a funnel.
It's thundering somewhere, the clouds are thundering!
The fortune teller directed her sleepy gaze
Straight at my child.

"What will you tell us?"
"Everything with no lies."
 "It's too late for me,
 Still too early for her..."
"Oh, hold your tongue, beauty!

What's the point saying before it's time: I don't believe it!"
And a black hand — all in silver —
Flashed open a playing card fan,

"Brazen in talk,
 Simple in character,
 You live a generous life
 Not hoarding your beauty.
 In a teaspoon of water — ah — a wicked man
 Will drown you.

 Soon in the night you'll have an unexpected path...
 The line is too short,
 Too little good-fortune."
 Make it golden!

And with a crash of thunder
A black — on black — ace sprouts.

May 19, 1917

*

You kiss the forehead — to wipe away fear.
I kiss the forehead.

You kiss the eyes — to take away sleeplessness.
I kiss the eyes.

You kiss the lips — to quench thirst.
I kiss the lips.

You kiss the forehead — to wipe away memory.
I kiss the forehead.

June 5, 1917

GYPSY WEDDING

Dirt flies
From beneath hooves.
Before my face
Is a shawl — like a shield.
Have a good time, matchmakers,
Without the young pair!
Hey, take us away from this trouble spot,
Shaggy steed!

Father and mother
Didn't give us our freedom,
Our wedding bed is —
The entire field for us.

Drunk without wine, sated without bread,
This is a gypsy wedding rushing by!

Glass's filled,
Glass's empty.
The guitar's rumble, the moon and dirt.

To the right and left the waist swayed.
The gypsy man — like a prince!
The prince — like a gypsy!
Hey, sir, be careful, it burns!
This is a gypsy wedding drinking!

There on a pile
Of shawls and fur coats,
The ringing and rustling
Of steel and lips.
Spurs jingled,
A coin necklace clinked as an answer.
Beneath someone's arm silk
Whistled.

Someone begins to howl like a wolf,
Someone is snoring like a bull.
  — This is a gypsy wedding asleep.

June 5, 1917

From
CRAFT
(1923)

MARINA TSVETAEVA

THE NOVICE

> *Tell me — what are you meditating about?*
> *Into the rain — beneath a single cape,*
> *Into the night — beneath a single cape, then*
> *Into a coffin — beneath a single cape.*

I

To be your fair-haired little boy,
 — O, across all the ages! —
To follow behind your dusty purple
Wearing the coarse cape of a novice.

Through all the human dregs to catch
Your life-giving sigh
With the soul, living by your breath
Like the blowing of a cape by — a gust of wind.

More victorious than King David
To move the mob aside with my shoulder.
From all insults, from all earthly offense
To serve you as your cape.

To be among sleeping novices
The one who does not sleep in sleep.
At the first stone raised by the mob
To be no longer a cape — but a shield!

(O, this line of verse is not interrupted on purpose!
The knife has become too sharp!)
And — smiling with inspiration — to be the first
To ascend onto your pyre.

April 15, 1921

2

There is a certain hour...
— Tiutchev[15]

There is a certain hour — that's like a cast-off burden:
When we curb the arrogance within us.
The hour of apprenticeship that in every life
Is triumphantly inescapable.

A lofty hour, when laying down weapons
To the feet of the one pointed out to us — by God's finger,
We exchange the purple of the Warrior
For camel hair on the ocean sand.

O, this hour, which like the Voice lifts us
to our deed — from the willfulness of days!
O this hour, when we stoop over
From our burden like a ripe ear of wheat.

And the grain has grown, and a blithe hour has struck,
And the seeds have craved millstones.
The law! The law! The yoke after which I lusted
When I was yet in the earthen womb.

The time of apprenticeship! But visible and knowable to us
Is another light, — another dawn has broken through.
Coming after it you are blessed —
You — the supreme hour of loneliness!

April 15, 1921

3

The sun of the Evening is – kinder
Than the sun at noon.
The sun is exceedingly cruel —
It doesn't warm at mid-day.

The sun approaching night
Is more aloof and meek.
Made wiser, it no longer wants
To beam into our eyes.

With its queen-like — anxiety-causing —
Simplicity,
The Evening Sun is dearer
To the singer of songs!

Crucified by the darkness
Every evening,
The sun of the Evening does not bow down
To the throng.

Overthrown from the throne
Don't forget — Phoebus!
The overthrown — does not look down —
But into the sky!

O, don't taper off on the neighboring
Bell tower!
I want to be your final
Bell tower.

April 16, 1921

6

All the splendor
Of trumpets is — just the babbling
Of grass — before Him.

All the splendor
Of storms is — just the chattering
Of birds before — You.

All the grandeur
Of wings is — just the trembling
Of eyelids before — You.

April 23, 1921

THE LEADER'S RETURN

The horse's lame,
The sword's rusty.
Who's this?
The leader of throngs.

A stride is — an hour,
A sigh is — a century,

MARINA TSVETAEVA

The gaze is — down,
All is — there.

An enemy. — A friend.
Thorns. — Laurels.
All is — a dream...
— He. — The horse.

The horse is — lame.
The sword is — rusty.
His cape is — ancient.
His stance is — straight.

July 16, 1921

From
AFTER RUSSIA
(1928)

*

There is an hour for those words.
From auditory stupors
Life taps out
Its lofty laws.

Perhaps — from the shoulder,
Pressed out by the brow.
Perhaps — from a ray
Unseen during the day.

Dust into a useless string —
An arm-waving leap onto a sheet.[16]
A tribute to your fear
And to your dust.

The hour of ardent arbitrariness
And the quietest requests.
The hour of landless brotherhoods
And worldwide orphanedness.

June 11, 1922

*

Nocturnal whispers: a hand
Strewing silks.
Nocturnal whispers: lips
Smoothing silks.
     Settling scores

Of all the daily jealousies —
    and the flaring up
Of all antiquities — clenching jaws —
And the argument
Quieted —
In a rustle...

And a leaf
Into a window...
And the first bird's whistle.
"So clear!" And a sigh.
Wrong one. Gone.
I left.
And the shudder
Of a shoulder.

Nothing.
Futility.
The end.
No trace.

And into this vanity of vanities
This sword: the dawn.

June 17, 1922

THE BALCONY

Ah, from an open precipice —
Down into dust and tar!
The shortweight of earthly love
To salt with a tear — for how long?

A balcony. The tar of wicked kisses
Through salty downpours.
And the sigh of unreceding hate:
To be breathed out into a line of verse!

Squeezed into the hand like a lump —
What: a heart or a cambric
Rag? For these lotions
There is a name: the Jordan.[17]

Yes, for this battle with love
Is wild and cruel hearted.
Having soared up from a granite brow —
To be breathed out into death.

June 30, 1922

TREES[18]

8

Someone rides — to mortal victory.
Trees have — the gestures of tragedies.
Judea's — sacrificial dance!
Trees have — the trembling of mysteries.

This is — a conspiracy against the age:
Against weight, counting, time, fractions.
Behold — a curtain torn to shreds:
Trees have the gestures of tombstones…

Someone rides. The sky is — like an entryway.
The trees have — the gestures of jubilations.
May 7, 1923

9

With what inspiration,
With what truths,
About what do you rustle?
Floods of leaves?

With which frantic Sibyl's
Mysteries —
About what do you rustle,
About what do you rave?

What is your wafting about?
But I know you cure
The hurt of Time —
With the cold of Eternity.

But like a young genius
Rising up — you discredit
The lie of beholding
With God's invisible finger.

So that anew, as once before,
The earth would *appear* to us,
So that *beneath eyelids*
Intentions can be fulfilled!

So that you do not boast
With the coins of miracles.
So that beneath eyelids
Mysteries come true.

Away from permanence!
Away from hurriedness!
Into the current! Into auguries
With indirect speech...

Is it foliage — like leaves?
Is it the Sibyl who has moaned herself out?
...Leafy avalanches,
Leafy ruins...

May 9, 1923

*

These are ashes of treasures:
Of losses, of hurts.
These are ashes before which
Granite turns — to dust.

A dove bare and bright
Not part of a pair.
Solomon's ashes above
The great earthly vanity.

And the threatening chalk
Of sunsetless time.

It means God entered my doors —
After the house burned down!

Not stifled in rubbish,
Master of my dreams and days,
The spirit like a steep flame
Arises from premature grays![19]

It is not you who betrayed me, years,
Behind my back!
This grayness is the victory
Of immortal powers.

September 27, 1922

OPHELIA TO HAMLET

Like Hamlet — laced up — tightly,
In the nimbus of dissuasion and knowledge,
Pale — to the last atom...
(From the edition of the year one thousand and what?)

With insolence and shallowness — don't touch!
(A teenager's attic stores!)
You have already lain — on this breast
Like some weighty chronicle,

Male virgin! Misogynist! Who prefers embracing
The foolish one... Did you think at least
Once about what — has been picked
In the flower bed of madness...

Roses?... But of course this is — hush! — The future!
We tear them — and new ones grow! Did the roses
Betray even once? The lovers —
Did they betray even once? Have they gone?

Having performed (having smelled sweetly) you will
drown...
— It never was! — But we will rise in memory
At the hour when above the stream's chronicle,
Like Hamlet — all laced up — you will rise...

February 28, 1923

OPHELIA — IN DEFENSE OF THE QUEEN

Prince Hamlet! Stop stirring up
The wormy sediments... Gaze at the roses!
Think of the one, who for the sake of just a single
day —
Counts her last days.

Prince Hamlet! Stop discrediting
The queen's womb... It's not for male virgins — to
judge
Passion. Phaedra's guilt is — grave.
Yet they sing of her till this day.

And will continue to be! — But You, with your
mixture of lime

And decay... Talk spitefully with the bones,
Prince Hamlet! With Your reason you cannot
Judge impassioned blood.[20]

But if... Then beware!... Through gravestones
Upward — into the bed chamber — to the heart's
content!
I stand to the defense of my queen —
I, Your immortal passion.
February 28, 1923

WIRES[21]

> *Des Herzens Woge schäumte nicht so schön empor, und würde Geist, wenn nicht der alte stumme Fels, das Schicksal, ihr entgegenstände.*[22]

I

In a row of singing pillars,
Supporting the Empyrean,[23]
I send to you my share
Of the dale's dust.
    Along the alley
Of sighs — with a wire to a pole —
A telegraphic: I lo — o — ve...

I plead... (a standard blank form
Won't fit it! It is simpler by wires!)
These are pillars, on them Atlas
Lowered a race track
Of Olympian gods...
      Along the pillars
A telegraphic fa — are — well...

Do you hear? This is the last straining[24]
Of a lost voice: fa — are — well...[25]
These are riggings above a sea of fields,
The quiet Atlantic path:

Higher, higher — and we mer — ged
In Ariadne's:[26] re — turn,

Turn around!.. The melancholy call
Of charity hospitals: I won't get out!
In the farewells of steel wires
Are the voices of Hades

Moving away... Conjuring
The distance: pi — ty...

Pity me! (In this chorus will you notice
It?) In the death rattle
Of obstinate passions is
The breath of Eurydice:

Through mounds — and — ditches
Eurydice's: a — a — las,

Don't lea —

March 17, 1923

6.

The hour when kings and gifts
Travel to one another above.
(The hour, when I walk from the mountain):
The mountains begin to understand.

Intentions heaped up into a circle.
Fates moved together: I won't betray you!
(The hour when I don't see hands)

Souls begin to see.

March 25, 1923

7.

At the hour when my dear brother
Passed the last elm tree
(the last in the line of waved farewells).
There were tears — larger than eyes.

At the hour when my dear friend
Sailed around the last cape

(Of mental sighs: return!), there were hands
Waving — wider than outstretched arms.

As though hands extended after you, all the way from the shoulder!
Like lips following after, — to cast a spell!
Speech lost sounds,
My hand lost fingers.

At the hour when my dear guest...
 — Lord, look at us! —
There were tears bigger than
Eyes and the Atlantic's
Stars...

March 26, 1923

IN PRAISE OF TIME

For Vera Arenskaya[27]

The refugee pavement!
It whooped and ran off
Like the headlong rush of wheels.
Time! I can't keep up with you.

Captured in chronicles and
In kisses... but rustling
In a small stream of sands...
Time, you will deceive me!

With clock hands, with ruts

Of wrinkles — and with America's
Novelties... — The jug is empty! —
Time, you will give me short measure!

Time, you will betray me!
Like an unfaithful wife — like a toy
You will drop me... — "Time is short, but it is ours!"

 — Your trains have a different
Destination!..

I have been born
Outside of time! In vain, in futility
You fight against it! A caliph for an hour:
Time! I will pass you!

May 10, 1923

DIALOGUE OF HAMLET WITH HIS CONSCIENCE

"She is at the bottom where there is silt
And seaweed... She went to sleep
Among it, but even there, there is no sleep!"
"But I loved her
As forty thousand brothers
Could not have loved her!"
            "Hamlet!

She is at the bottom where there is silt:
Silt!... And the last wreath
Came to the surface on driftwood..."

"But I loved her
As forty thousand..."
                "Less,

All the same, than one lover.
She is at the bottom where there is silt."
— "But was it she I —
               (*bewildered*)
                         — loved??"

June 5, 1923

THE CURTAIN

With a curtain's waterfalls, like foam —
Like a pine forest — like a flame — roaring by.
The curtain has no mystery from the stage:
(You are the stage, and I am the curtain).

With dream-like thickets (in the lofty
Hall confusion streamed forth)
I hide the hero in his struggle with Fate,
The place of action — and — the hour.

With waterfall rainbows, with the avalanche
Of laurels (after all, you entrusted yourself to me!
                                          you knew!)
I screen you from the hall,
(I enchant the hall!)

The mystery of the curtain! With the dream-like forest
Of sleepy potions, grasses, grains...

(Behind the already quivering drape
The pace of a tragedy — like — a storm!)

Loge seats, weep! Sound the alarm, balcony!
Appointed hour, come into being! Hero, be!
The curtain moves — like — a sail,
The curtain moves — like — a breast.

From the last heart, O bowels,
I screen you. — An outburst!
Over a stung Phaedra
The curtain rose — like — a vulture.[28]

Take it! Rant! Look! Isn't that blood?
Prepare the vat!
I will give my sovereign wound to the last drop!
(The spectator is white, the curtain glowing).

And then, with a compassionate cover
For the dale, roaring by like a banner.
The curtain has no mystery from the hall.
(The hall is life, and I am the curtain).

June 23, 1923

A MINUTE

A minute: passing: you will pass!
The same way both passion and friend pass by!
Today let's throw out what tomorrow
Would be torn out of our hands!

Minute: measuring! Giving measure
To the minuteness, hear me out:
That which ended
Never had begun. So lie, so flatter

Others still susceptible to a teenager's case
Of measles, who failed to grow up
Out of the way of things. Who are you
To squander the sea? The watershed

Of a living soul? O, shoal! O, trifle!
The glorious King of Bounties
Had no more glorious kingdom
Than the inscription: "This, too, shall pass"[29] —

On a signet ring... On backward paths
Who hasn't measured the vanity
Of your clock-face Arabias
And the pining of pendulums?

Minute: languishing! Illusion lingering
To gallop! Crushing us
Into dust and into trash You, Minute,
That will pass: alms for dogs!

O, how I am eager to leave that world
Where pendulums tear the soul,
Where the missed meeting of minutes
Rules my eternity.

August 12, 1923

THE PRAGUE KNIGHT[30]

Pale — faced
Guard above the lapping of the age —
Knight, knight,
Guarding the river.

(O, will I find in it
Peace from lips and hands?!)
Guar — di — an
On the watch of partings.

Oaths, rings...
Yes, but like a stone into the river —
How many of us
For four centuries!

The permit into the water
Is free. For the roses — to bloom!
He dumped me — I'll jump!
That is revenge for you!

We will not tire —
As long as there is passion!
To avenge with bridges.
Spread yourselves widely,

Wings! Into the mire
Into the foam — as though into brocade!
I won't pay
For the bridge's — blame today![31]

"Dare to jump down
From the fateful bridge!"
I am your height,
Prague knight.

Whether sweetness, whether sadness
Is in the river — you know better,
Knight guarding
The river of days.

September 27, 1923

NOCTURNAL PLACES

The darkest of nocturnal
Places: a bridge. — Lips to lips!
Really should we drag
Our cross to disreputable places,

There: into the laughing gas
Of gazes, of gauze... Into a Sodom that has a price?
Onto a bunk, where everyone has been!
Onto a bunk, where no one

Is alone... A night lamp dims.
Maybe — conscience will sleep!
(The truest of nocturnal
Places is death! Water is more blissful

Than — the nocturnal confinement that has a price!
Water is — smoother than bed sheets!

To love is — caprice and grief!
There — into the cold blue!

If only we could arise into the beliefs
Of the age! Having joined our arms!
(For the body the river is — light,
It is better to sleep than — to live!)

Love: a chill to the bone!
Love: white-hot heat!
Water loves — endings.
The river — loves bodies.

September 4, 1923

AN ATTEMPT AT JEALOUSY[32]

How is your life with another, —
Simpler, huh? — The stroke of an oar! —
Like the receding shoreline
The memory of me

Has gone quickly, me, a floating island
(In the sky — not on the water!)
Souls, souls! You should be sisters,
Not mistresses!

How is your life with a *common*
Woman? *Without* deities?
Since you overthrew Her Majesty
(Having yourself stepped down from the throne),

How is your life — busy —
Hemming and hawing? Getting up — how?
How do you cope, pauper,
With the customs duty of immortal triviality?

"Enough of convulsions and trembling —
Enough! I'll rent myself a house."
How is your life with just anyone —
My chosen one!

Is the food more suitable, tastier to eat?
When you are fed up — you have yourself to blame...
How is your life with an imitation —
You, who trampled over Mt. Sinai!

How's life with another's woman,
From this world? Loved — for being made from a rib?
Doesn't shame lash your brow
Like the rein of mighty Zeus?[33]

How's your life — how's your health —
Still able? How's your singing — eh?
How do you cope, pauper, with the wound
Of immortal conscience?

How's your life with market
Goods? Is the rent too steep?
After the marble of Carrara[34]
How is your life with plaster

Dust? (God was sculpted
From rubble — and smashed into bits!)

How is your life with the one-thousandth one —
You, who knew Lilith![35]

Are you sated with the market's novelty?
Having grown cold to magic,
How is your life with an earthly
Woman, without a sixth

Sense? Well, say there: are you mindlessly happy?
No? In an abyss without depth —
How is your life, my dear? Is it any harder,
Or is it the same as for me with another?

November 19, 1924

*

A scimitar? A fire?
More modest — why such big words!

It is pain, as familiar to the eyes as the palm,
As to lips —
The name of one's own child.

December 1, 1924

*

More ample than an organ's sound more jangling than
                                            a tambourine
Speech — and there is just one for all:

Oh, when it's hard, and *ah*, when it's marvelous,
And when it doesn't come easy — *eh*!

Ah from the Empyrean and *oh* over tilled fields,
And acknowledge, poet,
That the Muse has nothing
Other than these *ahs* and *ohs*.

The most saturated rhyme
Of deepest depths, the lowest tone.
This is Solomon's *ahing*
Before the blushing Shulamite.[36]

Ah: is a heart being torn apart,
The syllable on which you die.
Ah, is a curtain suddenly gaping open.
Oh: is a drayman's yoke.

A wordsearcher, a verbal rogue,
An open spigot of words,
Eh, if at least once you have heard —
The Polovtsian camp *ahing* in the night![37]

He bent down, and perked up like a beast...
Wrapped in moss, in the fur of the sound:
Ah is — for it's a gypsy camp
Entirely! — and with the moon above![38]

Behold a stallion, baring teeth a yard's width,
That neighs, anticipating a gallop.
This is Oleg, who stumbled across
His steed's skull, and commissioned Pushkin

To write a song.³⁹ And — glowing in flight —
In the great warriors'⁴⁰ darkness —
The invincible shouts of the flesh:
*Oh! — Eh! — Ah!*⁴¹

December 23, 1924

*

Dis — tance: mileposts, miles...⁴²
We were placed — apart, seated — separately,
So that we would quietly be
At two different ends of the earth.

Dis — tance: mileposts, far-off places...
They unglued us, unsoldered us,
Crucifying us, they separated our two hands,
But they didn't know that it was the fusion

Of inspiration and sinews...
They didn't set us at odds — they scattered us,
They split us apart...
        A wall and a ditch.
They displaced us like eagle-

Conspirators: mileposts, far-off places...
Didn't make us despair — they discarded us.
Along the slums of earthly latitudes
They shoved us into separate corners like orphans.

Which one, which one is it, already — March?!
They cut us — like a deck of cards!

March 24, 1925

FROM POEMS
NOT PUBLISHED IN COLLECTIONS

I like that you're lovesick not with me,
I like that I'm not lovesick with you,
That the heavy earthly sphere
Will never float off from beneath our feet.
I like that I can be amusing with you –
Be rakish with you – and not mince words,
And not blush in a stifling wave
When our sleeves slightly graze each other.

I also like that in my presence you
Can coolly hug someone else,
That you don't predict I'll burn in hellfire
For the fact that it's not you I'm kissing.
And that, my dear one, you don't mention
My dear name in the daytime or at night – in vain...
And that never in the silence of a church
Will they sing over us: an alleluiah![43]

Thank You with both heart and hand
For the fact that you — without knowing it yourself! —
Love me so: for my nighttime calm,
For the rarity of our sunset meetings,
For our non-strolls beneath the moon,
For the sun not above our heads,
For the fact that you're lovesick — alas! — not with me,
For the fact that I'm lovesick — alas! — not with you!

May 3, 1915

*

In the fatal folio
There is no temptation for
A woman. — *Ars Amandi*[44]
For a woman is the entire earth.

The heart is — the potion
Of love potions — surer than any other.
From the cradle on, a woman
Is someone's mortal sin.

Ah, how far to heaven!
Lips — close to yours in the fog...
"God, judge me not!" You've never been
A woman on this earth!

September 29, 1915

THE ACTOR[45]

2

You're so forgetful, yet so unforgettable.
–Ah, You look just like Your smile!
Say something else? – More beautiful than a golden morning!
Say something else? The only one in the entire Universe!
The prisoner of war of young Love itself,
A chalice cast by Cellini's hand.[46]

Friend, allow me in the age-old way
To declare love, the most tender in the world.
I love You. —In the fireplace the wind is howling.
Lounging – staring into the fireplace fire –
I love You. My love is innocent.
I'm saying it the way little children do.

Friend! All this will pass! —Temples pressed into palms, –
Life will unclench itself! —Love will release You,
A young prisoner of war, but – inspired –
My winged voice will prophesize to everyone –
About the fact that You once lived on this Earth –
So forgetful, yet so unforgettable!

End of November 1918

9

Your tender mouth is – nonstop kissing...
—And that's it; I'm totally like a beggar.
Who am I now? –The only one? –No, the thousandth!
A conqueror? –No, the conquered!

Whether this is love – or admiration,
The whim of a pen – or the reason,
Yearning to be an angel –
A bit of affection – by your calling...

–The sadness of the soul, the enchantment of the eyes,
The flourish of a pen – ah! – it doesn't really matter,
What you will call these lips – as long as
Your tender mouth is – nonstop kissing!
                              December 1918

17

Mortal lips and mortal arms
Have blindly destroyed my eternity.
With my eternal Soul in separation—
I sing the mortal lips and arms.

The rumbling of divine eternity is – more muffled.
Only at times at the break of day –
From the dark heavens – a mysterious voice utters:
–Woman! –Remember your immortal soul!
                              The end of December 1918

GRAY HAIR

These are ashes of treasures:
Of losses, affronts.
These are ashes before which
Granite turns — to dust.

A bare and bright dove
Not living as a pair.
Solomon's ashes
Above the great vanity there.

The threatening chalk
Of sunsetless time.
It means God entered my doors
After the house burned down!

Not stifled in rubbish,
Master to dreams and days,
Like a sheer flame
Spirit comes – from the premature gray!

And it is not you who betrayed me,
Years — go to the rear!
This grayness is the victory
Of immortal powers.

September 27, 1922

*

Quieter, praise!
Don't slam the door,
Glory!

Table's
Corner — and an elbow.

A commotion, stop!
Heart, give it a rest!
An elbow — and forehead.
An elbow — and a thought.

Youth is — for loving,
Old age — for keeping warm:
No time — *to be*,
Nowhere to go.

At least a nook —
Just without others!
Spigots — leak,
Chairs — thunder,

Mouths speak:
Mumbling with marbles
In the mouth
Give thanks "for beauty."

If only you knew,
Near and far one,
How much I pity
My own head —

Like God in the Horde!
The steppe's — a casemate —
Paradise — this is where
They *do not* speak!

A womanizer's — a swine —
A storekeeper's just — a detail!
God for me will be the one
Who'll give me

— Not the time! —
My days are numbered—
But four walls
For silence's sake.

Paris January 26, 1926

THE POET AND TSAR[47]

I

With the otherworldly
Hall of tsars.
  — What about this one of marble,
 The unbending one?

So magnificent
In the gold of the shoulder mantle.
  — A pitiful gendarme
Of Pushkin's glory.[48]

He cursed — the author,
He cut — the manuscript.
The vicious butcher
Of the Polish land.[49]

Look more sharp-eyed!
Don't you ever forget:
The killer of singers
Tsar Nicholas
The First.

July 12, 1931

*

I opened my veins: indefatigably,
Irretrievably life gushes out.
Set out the bowls and plates!
Each and every plate will be too shallow,
The bowl — too flat.

Over the edge — and *past it* —
Into the black earth, to nourish a reed,
Irreversibly, indefatigably,
Irretrievably lines of poetry gush out.

January 6, 1934

POEM OF THE MOUNTAIN
(1924)

POEM OF THE MOUNTAIN

> *Liebster, Dich wundert*
> *die Rede? Alle Scheidenden*
> *reden wie Trunkne und*
> *nehmen gerne sich festlich...50*
> — Hölderlin

DEDICATION

You shudder — mountains drop from your shoulders,
And the soul — ascends.
Let me sing of my mounting grief:
Of my mountain!

I will not plug up the dark hole
Not today nor tomorrow.
Let me sing of my mounting grief
At the top of the mountain.

I

That mountain crest was like the chest
Of a recruit, felled by a shell.
That mountain wanted *virgin*
Lips, that mountain demanded

A wedding ceremony.
 — The ocean into the cochlea
With a suddenly breaking-in *hurrah*! —
That mountain spurred and warred.

That mountain was like thunder!
We flirt with titans in vain
(Do you remember the last house
Of that mountain — at the edge of the city limits?)

That mountain was — worlds!
God charges dearly for the world![51]
Mourning began from the mountain.
That mountain above the city.

2

Not Parnassus, not the Sinai,
Just a bare barracks
Hill, — Line up! Fire! —
Why then for my eyes
(Since it's October now, not May)
Was that mountain Paradise?

3

Like a paradise offered
On a palm — don't touch it if it's burning!
The mountain threw itself under our feet
In the ruts of slopes.

As though with a titan's paws
Of bushes and needles —
The mountain grabbed us by the hems
And ordered us: Stop!

O, it's far from being an ABC-primer of
Paradise — a draft of drafts!
The mountain knocked us on our back,
It commanded us: lie down!

Struck dumb beneath the onslaught
 — How? You can't figure it out even today! —
The mountain, like a matchmaker of — holiness,
Pointed: here...

4

The pomegranate seed of Persephone,[52]
How can I forget you in the frosts of winter?
I remember lips like a double seashell
Partly opening up to mine.

Persephone, ruined by a seed,
The persistent crimson of lips,
And the spaces between your eyelashes — like notches,
And the golden point of a star.

5

Passion's not a deception, or figment of imagination!
It doesn't lie — just don't prolong it!
O, if only we'd appear in this world
As commoners of love!

O, if only with common sense and in simple terms:
Just — a hill, just — a mound...
They say — you measure the height of a mountain
By your attraction toward the abyss.

In heaps of brown heather,
In islands of afflicted pine needles...
(The height of delirium — above the level
Of life)
    — Here take me! I'm yours...

Rather the quiet cordialities of the family,
Rather the babbling of nestlings — alas!
Because we appeared in this world —
As celestial beings of love!

6

The mountain mourned (but mountains mourn
With bitter clay in the hours of parting),
The mountain mourned about the dovelike
Tenderness of our unheralded mornings.

The mountain mourned over our friendship:
The most constant kinship of lips!
The mountains spoke that everyone
Will receive — according to *his tears*.[53]

The mountain also mouthed that life
Is a gypsy camp, that you squandered your life
                                      in different hearts!
The mountain also mourned: you could at least
Let Hagar and her child go![54]

And it also said this is a demon that
Is twisting and turning, that there is no plan to
                                              the game.
The mountain spoke. We were mute
We let the mountain judge.

7

The mountain mourned that it will become only
Sorrow — that today there is only blood and torrid heat.
The mountain mourned that it will not release
Us, not let you be with another woman.

The mountain mourned that it will become
Just smoke — that today: it will be both peace
                                              and Rome.
The mountain mouthed that we are to be
With another (I don't envy them!).

The mountain mourned over the awful burden
Of an oath, that was too late to be cursed.
The mountain said that the Gordian Knot is —
Just too old — duty and passion.

The mountain mourned over our mourning:
Tomorrow! Not right away! When above the brow —
There already is no *memento*, but just — *mori*![55]
Tomorrow, when we will understand!

The sound...well is it as though someone
Is crying...somewhere nearby?
The mountain mourned that we have to go down
Separately, through this dirt —

Into a life, of which we all know:
The mob — the market — the barracks.
The mountain also said that all poems
Of mountains — are written — *like this*.

8

That mountain was like the hunched back
Of Atlas, a moaning titan.
Prague will be proud of that mountain
The city where from morning to night we

Trump our life — like a card!
We passionate people persist *in not being*.
In the same mold as the bear moat[56]
And the twelve apostles —

Revere my gloomy grotto,
(I was — that grotto, and the waves splashed in!)
Do you remember the last move
Of that game — at the edge of the suburbs?

That mountain was — worlds!
Gods take revenge against their imitations!
....
Mourning began from the mountain.
That mountain on me is — a tombstone.

9

Years will pass. And — the above-mentioned
Stone will be removed, replaced by a flat one.[57]
They will cover our mountain with *dachas*,
They will clutter it with little garden plots.

They say that in these kind of outlying areas
The air's cleaner and it's easier to live.
And they'll start to carve up the land into lots,
And dazzle you with crossbeams of the *dachas*,

To smooth out my mountain gaps,
All my ravines — turn bottom's up!
After all — for someone
Homes are — happiness, and *happiness* to the home!

Happiness — at home! Love without delusions!
Without the stretching of sinews!
I need to be a woman — and endure!
(There used to be happiness when he used to come,

Happiness — in the home!) The city of love,
Brightened up neither by parting or a knife
Will rise on the ruins
Of our happiness: the city of husbands and wives.

And in that blessed air,
 — While you still can — be sinful! —
There will be shopkeepers resting
To chew up the profits,

To think up floors and passages,
So that every thread — would be used for the house!
For somebody after all needs
A roof with a stork's nest.[58]

10

But beneath the weight of those foundations
The mountain will not forget — the game.
The mountain has — mountains of time:
It has those gone astray, but not those memory-free!

Along the unrepentant fissures
A vacationer will grasp it too late:

This is not a knoll, overgrown with families —
But a crater, set into rotation!

You can't fetter Vesuvius
With grapevines! You can't bind a giant
With hemp! Just the madness
Of lips is — enough for the vineyards

To begin to stir like a lion's mane,
Pouring out the lava of hate.
Your daughters will be strumpets
And your sons — poets!

Daughter, raise a child out of wedlock!
Son, ruin yourself with gypsy women!
There will be no den of iniquity,
For you, bodies, on my blood!

With an oath of a man on his death-bed,
An oath stronger than a cornerstone, I swear:
You will have no earthly happiness,
Ants, upon the heights of my mountain!

At an unknown hour, at an unknown date,
You will comprehend with all your family
The foolhardy and massive
Mountain of the seventh commandment![59]

AN AFTERWORD

There are blank spots in memory — cataracts
On the eyes: seven veils.
I don't remember you separately.
Instead of features — a white precipice.

Without marks. Entirely — like a single
Blank spot. (The soul, covered with wounds,
Is — one continuous wound.) To mark the details
With chalk is the business of tailors.

The firmament is created as an integral piece.
Is the ocean — an amassment of splashes?!
With no distinguishing features. Probably — entirely —
Special. Love is a bond, not an investigation.

I don't know whether you're black-haired — or fair —
Let the neighbor tell me: he can see.
Can passion really — divide you into separate pieces?
Am I a watchmaker or a surgeon?

You, like a circle, are complete and unbroken.
An *entire* whirlwind, a *complete* stupor.
I don't remember you separately
From love. It's the sign of equality.

(In the piles of dreamy down:
A waterfall, mounds of foam —
With novelty, strange to the ear:
Instead: "I" — the royal: "we"...)

But on the other hand, in a beggarly and cramped
Life: "life, as it is" —
I don't see you together
With anyone:
     — revenge to memory.
January 1-February 1, 1924
Prague. The Mountain.

POEM OF THE END
(1924)

POEM OF THE END

1

In a sky, rustier than tin-plate,
The finger of a pillar.
He stood at the appointed place,
Like fate.

"Quarter-to. On time?"
"Death doesn't wait."
Exaggeratedly-smooth
The sweeping tip of his hat.

In each eyelash — a challenge.
Mouth taut.
His bow
Exaggeratedly low.

"Quarter-to. On the dot?"
The voice lied.
My heart sank: what's with him?
The brain: a signal!

―――――

A sky of bad omens:
Rust and tin-plate.
He waited at the usual place,
The time: six.

This kiss was without a sound:
The stupor of lips.
This way one kisses a queen's hand,
As well as the dead...

A commoner rushing
Jabbed his elbow — into my side.
Exaggeratedly-drearily
The whistle howled.

It howled the way a dog yelps,
It went on, getting angry.
(The exaggeration of life
 In the hour of death.)

What yesterday was only up to your waist,
Suddenly — reaches the stars.
(Exaggeratedly, that is:
In its entire height.)

Mentally: darling, darling.
"The hour? Past six,
To the cinema, or?..."
A blast: Home!

2

A gypsy camp brotherhood —
That's where it's led!
Like thunder out of the blue,
Like a saber withdrawn,

With all the horrors
Of words we wait for,
Like a collapsing house —
The word: home.

———

The shriek of a lost, spoiled
Child: home!
A year-old child:
"Give it to me!" "It's mine!"

My brother in debauchery,
My chill and my heat,
Some try to get away from home,
The way you strive to go home!

———

Like a horse tearing its tether —
Upward! — and the rope becomes dust.
"But there's no house!"
"There is, just ten steps away:

The house on the mountain." "Isn't it higher up?"
"The house at the mountain top.
With a window just under the roof.
"*Burning not just from the*

Dawn?" This way life starts once
Again? The simplicity of poems!
A home, that means: leaving the house
At night.
          (O, to whom will I tell

My sorrow, my misfortune,[60]
My terror, greener than ice?..)
"You've been thinking too much."
In response a pensive: "Yes."

3

And — it's an embankment. I keep to
The water, as though to a solid mass.
The Gardens of Semiramis hanging[61] —
Here you are!

I keep to the water's edge —
The steel strand with a corpse's pallor —
Like a singer to a sheet of music —
Like a blind man – to the edge

Of a wall...[62] You won't give it back?
No? I'll lean over the edge — will you hear?
I keep to the all-quencher of thirst,[63]
Like a sleep-walker to the edge

Of a roof...
     But my trembling is not because
Of the river — a naiad gave birth to me!
Keep to the river the way you keep to a hand
When your love is next to you —

And he's faithful...
           The dead are faithful.
Yes, but not to everyone in a small room...
Death on the left side, on the right side —
You. My right side is like a dead man.

A sheaf of striking rays of light.
 Laughter, like the sound of a cheap tambourine.
"You and I should..."
                (A chill.)
"Will we be brave?"

4

The flow of white-haired
Fog — in a gauze flounce.
Overfilled with exhalations, overfilled with smoke,
But mainly — with words spoken *ad infinitem*!
What does it smell of? Of extreme haste,
Indulgence and little sins:
With commercial secrets
And dance floor powder.

Married bachelors
Wearing rings, respectable young men...
Overfilled with scolding, overfilled with ridicule,
But mainly — with what was counted out!
Both with big bills, and small bills,
With telltale feathers in a tiny snout.[64]

...With commercial transactions
And dance floor powder.

(Half-turned: is *this* —
Our house? "But I'm not the lady of it!")
One — over a checkbook,
Another — over a gloved hand,
And yet another — over a foot in a lacquered shoe
Works on the sly.
...With commercial marriages
And dance floor powder.

Like a silver notch
In the window is — a Maltese Star!
Over-caressed, over-loved a lot,
And mainly — over-squeezed!
Over-pinched... What can you do,
yesterday's leftovers: stink!)
...With commercial hanky-panky
And dance floor powder.

Is the chain too short?
On the other hand, it's not steel, but platinum!
Trembling with a triple
Chin, sacrificial cows chew on
Veal. Above a sugary little neck
The devil is — like a gas burner.
...With commercial crashes
And Berthold Schwartz's[65] —
Special powder...
                    He was
Talented — and a defender of the people.

"We need to talk to each other."
Will we be brave?

5

I capture the movement of lips.
And know — he won't say it first.
"You don't love me?" "No, I do."
"You don't love me!" "But I'm torn to pieces,

Drunk up, tormented."
(Like an eagle gazing at the terrain):
"Excuse me, is *this* — a home?
"Home is — in my heart." Semantics!

Love is flesh and blood.
Color is — watered by one's own blood.
Do you think that love is
Chatting across a table for two?

For just an hour — then each of us goes home?
Like those gentlemen and ladies?
Love, that means...
                —A shrine?
Child, replace it with a scar

On a scar! — "Under the gaze of servants
And revelers?" (I, without a sound:
"Love — means a bow,
A stretched bow: parting").

"Love means — a bond."
We have everything torn asunder: our mouths
                                        and our lives.
(I begged you: don't hex it!
At that hour, innermost, and so near,

That hour at the top of the mountain
And passion. A *memento* — gone like mist:
Love is — all the gifts tossed
Into a bonfire, and always, for naught!)

The shell's slit of the mouth
Is pale. Not a smile — an inventory.
"First and foremost just one
Bed."
      "Did you want to say

A chasm?" A drum roll
 Of the forefinger.
"It's not like moving mountains!"
Love means...
         "Mine."
I understand you. Conclusion?

———————

The drum roll of forefingers
 Intensifies. (A scaffold and city square.)
"Let's go away." And I: let's die,
I hoped. That's simpler!

Enough of cheapness:
Of Rhymes, rails, rooms, train stations...
"Love, that means: life."
"No, it was called

Something else by the ancients...
             "So?"
                           A piece
Of a kerchief in a fist like a fish.
"So are we going? Your route?"
Poison, rails, a piece of lead — your choice!

Death — and no arrangements!
"Life!" Like a Roman commander,
Gazing like an eagle at the remnants of
His armies.
       "Then let's say good-bye."

6

"I didn't want this.
Not this. (Silently: listen!
To want — that is the business of bodies,
But from this day on for one another

We are souls...) — And he didn't speak.
(Yes, at the hour when the train is announced,
You hand the sad honor of departure
To women like a

Glass of wine...) "Maybe it's delirium?
You didn't hear it right? (The courteous liar
Delivering the bloody honor
Of the break-up to his lover

Like a bouquet...)." Attentively: syllable
After syllable, and so — let's say good -bye,
You said? (Like a handkerchief
Dropped at the hour of sweet

Debauchery...) "You are the Caesar
Of this battle. (O, brazen thrust!
To return the sword surrendered
By a foe to that same

Foe!)" He continues. (A ringing
In the ears...) I bow down twice:
For the first time he's outstripped
In breaking up. "Do you say this to every woman?"

Don't deny it! Revenge
Worthy of Lovelace.[66]
A gesture, giving you honor,
But to me, pulling the meat

From my bones. — A chuckle. Through jest —
Death. A gesture. (No desires.
To want is the business — of *those*,
But from here on we are — shadows

For each other...) The last nail is
Nailed. A screw, because it's a lead coffin.

"The final of my last requests."
"Go ahead." "Never a word

About us... to anyone from... well...
Those who come after. " (From stretchers
This way the wounded enter — spring!)
"I'd ask you to do the same."

Give you a ring to remember me by?
"No." His widely gaping glance
Is absent. (Like a seal
Over your heart, like a seal

On your hand...[67] No scenes!
I'll swallow it.) More alluringly and quieter:
"How about a book for you?" "Like you give everybody?
No, don't write them at all.

Books..."

———————

It means, no need.
It means, no need.
No need to cry.

In our wandering
Fisherman's brotherhoods
We dance — but don't cry.

We drink, but don't cry.
With burning blood
We pay — but don't cry.

We dissolve a pearl
In a glass — and rule[68]
The world — but don't cry.

"So I'll go away?" — I gaze through
Him. Harlequin, for fidelity,
To his Pierrette — like a bone to a dog
Throwing the most despicable

Of primacies: the honor of the end,
The gesture of the curtain. The last
Locution. An inch of lead
Into the chest: it would be better, hotter

And — cleaner...
         I dug
My teeth into my lips.
I won't cry.

The very firmness —
Into the flesh.
Just not to cry.

In the wandering brotherhoods
We die, but don't cry,
We burn, but don't cry.

Into ashes and song
They hide the dead man
In wandering brotherhoods.

"So I'm the first? Mine is the first move?
You mean, like in chess? But after all,
They even ask us to go first
Onto a scaffold..."
                    "Urgently

I ask, don't look!" A look —
(Tears are about to roll down!
How do you chase them back
Into the eyes?!) — "I'm saying, don't

Stare!!!"

Distinctly and loudly
A gaze fixed into the heights:
"Let's go, darling,
 Or I'll start crying!"

———

I forgot! Among the living
Money-boxes (merchants — too!)
A blond flashed the back of his head:
Maize, corn, rye!

Washing away all the commandments
Of the Sinai — the fur of a maenad!
A horsehair cloth Holkonda,[69]
A treasure house of delights —

(For everyone!) It's not for nothing nature
Stockpiles, it's not that totally greedy!

From these blond tropics,
Hunters are — where is the path

Back? With vulgar nakedness
Teasing and blinding to the point of tears —
It spilled over with nothing but this golden
Laughing lustful lovemaking.[70]

— Isn't it true? — A clinging,
Crumpling stare. In each eyelash there is — an itch.
— And most importantly — this thickness!"
A gesture, twisting me into a wisp.

O, a gesture already showing ripping garments
Off! It's easier than drinking and eating —
A grin! (There's hope for you,
Alas, for salvation!)

Both sisterly and brotherly?
In alliance: a union!
— Not laying to rest — to laugh!
(And having laid to rest — I laugh.)

7

Then — the embankment. Last one.
That's it. Separately and without hands,
Like neighbors shunning one another
We plod along. From the river —

Crying. Without cares I lick off
The salty plunging quicksilver:
The heavens did not dispatch
Solomon's enormous moon to the tears.[71]

A pillar. Why not bang your head against it
Till it bleeds? Into smithereens, not till it bleeds!
Like fretting criminal accomplices
We ramble along. (What is killed is — love.)

Stop it! Is this really two lovers?
Into the night? Separately? To sleep with others?
"Do you understand that the future
Is in this?" I fall all the way back.

"To sleep!" Like newlyweds walking over their
                                                            bedside rug...
"To sleep!" We can't walk in step,
To the same beat. Plaintively: "Take me by the hand!
We're not convicts to act this way!..

An electric shock. (He lay on my arm as though
With his *soul*! — His hand on my hand.) The current
Pulses, in feverish wires
It tears — he lay on my soul with his hand!

He clings. Everything is iridescent! What is more
Iridescent than tears? Rain, like a bead curtain,
Closer spaced than the beads. "I don't know these kinds
                                               of embankments
That come to an end. — The bridge, and:
                                            "Well?

Here?" (The hearse has arrived).
The flight upward of peace — ful
Eyes. "Can I walk you home?"
For the fin — al time!

8

The fin — al bridge.
(I won't give back his hand, I won't pull mine away!)
The final bridge,
The final bridge of blame.

Wa — ter[72] and firmament.
I take out the coins.
A co — in[73] for death,
Charon's toll for crossing the Lethe.

The shadow of a co — in
In a shadowy hand. Those co — ins have
No sound.
Thus the shadow of a co — in

Into a shadowy hand.
Without reflection or jingling.
The co — ins are for them.
For the dead poppies will be enough.

A bridge.
_____

The bles — sed part
Of lovers without hope:
Bridge, you are like passion:
A convention: a complete in-between.

I'm nesting: warm,
Is the rib — that's why I cling to it so hard.
Neither *before* nor *afterward*:
An interlude of insight!

No arms or legs.
With all my bones and my entire thrust:
Only my side is alive,
Which I press against the one next to me.

All life is in this side!
It is an ear as well as — an echo.
I cling like a yolk to the egg white,
like a Samoyed to fur

I crowd to it, I stick to it,
I pave the way to it. Siamese twins,
What is your union compared to ours?
Do you remember — that woman: you called her

Mother? And having forgotten all and
Everything, in an immobile exultation
Carrying y — ou,
She didn't hold you any closer.

Understand it! We've lived like one together!
We've come true! You lullabied me on your chest!

I won't — jump down!
To dive — I'd have to let go of your hand

In – stead. I press tighter and tighter...
And I'm inseparable.
Bridge, you're not my husband:
A lover — a complete miss!

Bridge, you are on our side!
We feed the river with our bodies!
I've bitten into your life like ivy,
Like a tick: rip me out by the roots!

Like ivy! like a tick! —
Godlessly! Inhumanly!
Du – mp me, — like a thing,
Me who didn't respect

A single thing in this
Hollow, material world!
Tell me it's a dream!
That it's night, and after night — it's morning,

The Ex — press train and we're in Rome!
In Granada? I don't know myself,
Having tossed away the Mt. Blancs
And Himalyas of feather beds.

The cha — sm is too vast:
I warm you up with my last blood.
Lis — ten to my side!
This is surely truer

Than ver—ses... Aren't you
Warmed up? To whom will you sell yourself in
                                  the morning?
Te — ll me this is a delirium!
That there's not and never will be an end

To the bri — dge...
            — The end.
———————

— Here? —A divine, childlike
  Gesture. —Well? — I've sunk my teeth in.
— Ju —st a little more:
For the last time!"

9

With the factory buildings, booming
And responsive to the call...
The innermost secret from under the tongue of
Wives from husbands, and of widows

From friends — to you, the innermost
Secret of Eve from the tree — here it is:
I'm no more than an animal
Wounded in the gut by someone.

It burns... As though my soul's been torn out
With the skin! The notorious

Nonsensical heresy called the soul
Left through a hole like steam.

Pale Christian feebleness!
Steam! Plaster it with poultices!
It never was after all!
There was just a body, the body wanted to live,

———————

It doesn't want to live anymore.

Forgive me! I didn't want to!
The wail of ripped open bowels!
This way the condemned wait for the firing squad
At three in the morning

Playing chess... With a smile
Teasing the corridor's peephole.
We're just chess pawns!
And somebody plays us.

Who? Benevolent gods? Thieves?
As big as a peephole's eyelet —
An eye. The clank of
The red corridor. A bar's lifted up.

A puff on a shag of tobacco.
A spitting, so we've lived it up, spitting.
...Along these checkerboard pavements is
A straight road: into a ditch

And into blood. A secret eye:
The moon's listening peephole...
....
And looking sideways:
"How far away you are already!"

10

A shared shudder
In unison. "Our dairy bar café!"

Our island, our temple,
Where in the morning we were —

Part of the riff-raff! A short-lived pair! —
We celebrated our matins.

With the bazaar and vile stench
Permeated through with a dream and with spring...
Here the coffee was foul —
As though it were made entirely of oats!

(To extinguish capriciousness
With oats in racehorses!)
That coffee hardly smelled
Of Arabia,

But of Arcadia...

How the waitress smiled at us,
Seating us next to each other,

With a worldly and compassionate —
Guarded smile of

Gray-haired mistresses:
You will wither away! Live!
She smiled at our madness, at pennilessness,
At a yawn and at love, —

But mainly — at our youth!
At a chuckle — without reason,
At a grin — without intent,
At a face — without wrinkles —

O, mainly — at our youth!
At passions wrong for this climate!
Youth that has wafted — from somewhere,
That has poured in — from somewhere

Into the dim cafe:
— A burnouse and Tunis! —
Smiled at hopes and muscles
Beneath the decrepitude of raiments...

(Dear friend, I'm not complaining:
A scar on top of a scar!)
O, how the hostess
Saw us off in a starched

Dutch bonnet...

———

Not quite recalling, not quite understanding,
As though we were taken away from a celebration...
— Our street! — Now it's not ours anymore... —
—So many times along it... — No longer we... —

— Tomorrow the sun will rise in the west!
— David will break up with Jehovah!

— What are we doing? — Par — ting.
— That most stupid of words

Means nothing to me:
We are par — ting. — One out of a hundred?[74]
Just a word with two syllables
Behind which there is a void.

Stop! Is it Serbian or Croatian,
I guess, is it the Czech country going crazy in us?
Par — ting. To part...
What super-most-natural of nonsense!

The sound from which ears explode,
They stretch beyond the limit of longing...
Par — ting — it's not in the Russian tongue!
Not in the woman's! Not in the man's!

Not in God's! What are we — sheep,
Yawning at suppertime?
Par — ting — in what language?
There's no such meaning,

Not even a sound! It's simply the dull
Noise — of a saw, for example, through a dream.
Par — ting — is just a nightingale's moan,
That of the swan of Khlebnikov's

School... [75]
        But how did it turn out this way?
Like a dried up reservoir —
The air! You can hear a hand touching a hand.
To part — this is surely thunder

Out of the blue... This is the ocean dashing into a cabin.
The outermost cape of Oceania!
These streets are too steep:
To part — this surely is going down

A mountain... This is the sigh of soles
Weighing a ton...[76] A palm, finally, and a nail!
A reason that knocks you down:
To part — this is really separately, isn't it,

But we've grown into one...

11

To lose everything right away —
It couldn't be tidier.
Countryside, suburb:
An end to the days.

To bliss (read — to stones),
To the days, to the houses, to us.

Empty *dachas*! I revere them
The same way — as I did my old mother.

This surely is action — to stand empty:
What is hollow doesn't stay empty.

(*Dachas*, a third of you empty,
Better for you to burn down!)

Just don't shudder
Having opened the wound.
Countryside, countryside,
A tearing of sutures!

For without superfluous words,
Ornate ones — love is a suture.

A suture, and not a bandage, a suture — not a shield.
"O, don't beg for shelter!"
A suture by which the dead are stitched to the earth,
By which I'm stitched to you.

(Time will still show with which stitch:
A light one or three—ply!)

One way or another, my friend — arms at attention!
Into smithereens and slivers!
Only that of glory that has burst:
It's burst but didn't come apart at the seams!

Under the tacking thread — is a living red
Vein and not decay.

O, the one who breaks off
Doesn't lose!
The countryside, the suburb:
A divorce for brows.

They're executing nowadays in the
Villages — a draft of wind for brains!

O, one who walks away doesn't lose
At the hour when the dawn breaks.
I stitched a whole life for you
During the night, from scratch.

So don't reproach me for it being crooked:
The suburb is: — a rip for sutures.

Untidied up souls —
Are covered with scars!..

The countryside, the suburb:
The furious span

Of the suburb. With the boot of fate,
Do you hear it — along the moist clay?
...Blame it on my quick hand,
Friend, and the tenacious living

Thread — whichever way you damn it!
The fin — al lamp—post!

———

Here? A look is — just like —
A conspiracy. The look —
Of the lower races. "Can we go up the mountain?
For the fin — al time!"

12

Like a thick mane
Rain in our eyes. — Hills.
We passed the suburbs.
We're in the countryside.

There is — and isn't for us!
A stepmother — not a mother!
Nowhere to go further.
Here we'll pack it in.

A field. A fence.
We stand like brother and sister.
Life is a suburb. —
You must build outside the city!

Eh, a lost
Court case, ladies and gentlemen!
Everything there is nothing but suburbs!
Where are the cities?!

The rain rips and
Rages. We stand and rip.

For the past three months
The first time together!

And what did God want
To borrow from Job?
It just didn't come off:
We're outside of town!

Outside of town! Understand? Outside!
Out of it! Having walked across the rampart!
Life is a place where it's impossible to live:
A Jew — ish quarter...

Isn't it a hundred times more commendable
To become the Wandering Jew?[77]
Because for anyone who isn't a scum
Life is a Jew — ish —

Pogrom. It's alive only through converts!
By the Judases of faith!
To islands for lepers!
To hell! — anywhere! — but not to

Life, — it tolerates only converts — only
Sheep — to give them to a butcher!
With my fe — et I trample
My right to residence!

I trample! — Revenge
For David's shield! — Into the mash of bodies!
Isn't it thrilling that the Yid
Didn't want — to live?!

The ghetto of chosenness! A rampart and moat.
Don't expect any mer — cy!
In this most Christian of worlds
The poets are Yids!

13

This way knives are sharpened on a stone,
This way the shavings are swept
By brooms. Beneath hands
There is something furry, wet.

Where are you, my twins:
This masculine dryness, power?
Beneath a palm are —
Tears, not rain!

About what other temptations
Are we talking about? Property is like water!
After your diamond eyes
Pouring beneath my palm,

There is no death
For me. An end to the end!
I stroke — I stroke —
I stroke your face.

All us Marinas have such
Arrogance, — we, the Polish women.[78]
After your eagle's eyes,
Crying beneath your palm...

Are you crying? My friend!
All is mine! Forgive me!
O, how large tears are
And salty in my hand!

A man's tear is cruel:
The blunt part of an ax to the head![79]
Cry, with others you'll make up
The embarrassment you lost with me.

We are — fish from — the same
Sea! A wave of a hand:
...Like a dead shell
Lips on lips.

———————

Covered with tears.
A saltbush
To your taste.
"But what will it be
Tomorrow when
I wake up?"

14

Like a sheep's trail —
Down. The din of the city.
Three girls coming toward us.
Laughing. Laughing

At our tears — with all the afternoon
Of their depths, with the sea's crest!
They're laughing!
               — at those inappropriate,
Shameful, male

Tears of yours, visible
Through the rain — in two rows of sutures!
As though — at shameful pearls
On the bronze of a warrior.

At your first tears,
At your last — o, pour them out! —
At your tears — the pearls
In my crown!

I don't visibly lower my eyes.
Through the downpour — I stare.
Venus' dolls,
Stare! This union

Is closer than just
Allure and the bed.
Speech is replaced for us
By the Song of Songs itself.

To us, to unknown birds,
Solomon bows down
To the ground — for this shared
Lament is more than a dream!

———

And into the hollow waves
Of gloom — hunched over and equal —
Without trace — silently — you leave
The way a ship sinks.

Prague, February 1 —
Ilovishchi, June 8, 1924

Endnotes

1   The note echoes a passage in Song of Songs 8:6: "ibo krepka, kak smert', liubov'" (for love is strong as death; King James version).

2   Tsvetaeva's birthday.

3   A cycle of 17 poems dedicated to Tsvetaeva's lover in 1914-15, the poet Sophia Parnok (1885-1933).

4   "He-Him" is presumably Tsvetaeva's husband Sergei Efron.

5   The cemetery is located in the Krasnaya Presnya district of Moscow in the northwest part of the city. Many well-known Russian cultural figures are buried there.

6   Although the word "shal'noe" primarily means "wild," we feel that Tsvetaeva is playing with the word for "shawl" (*shal'*) in Russian here and creating an adjectival neologism from it. Akhmatova often wore a shawl. In perhaps the most famous portrait of her by Natan Altman in 1914, she is wearing a yellow shawl. Note also Tsvetaeva's 1916 poem "To Akhmatova," in which she writes: "A shawl from Turkish lands/Has fallen like a cloak." We have opted for the literal meaning of the word here, but the echoed meaning seems to fit Tsvetaeva's penchant for word play. The echoed reading of the line would be "shawled offspring of the white night."

7   Tsvetaeva is referring to Akhmatova being a Petersburg poet—on the backdrop of the city's famous white nights in June. "Rus" is the old name for the civilization that had its origins in present-day Kyiv, Ukraine as its capital. Akhmatova was born and raised in Kyiv. The Church of the Savior in Blood is one of the landmark churches of St. Petersburg: it was built on the spot where Tsar Alexander I was assassinated in 1861. Tsvetaeva is a Moscow poet with the cupolas of the Kremlin churches as one of the main landmarks of *her* city.

8   "Proshchenyi den'" suggests "Proshchenyi vtornik" – Shrove Tuesday (the day before Lent begins) or "Proshchenoe voskresen'e" (Shrove Sunday), the Sunday before Lent begins. On that day all Orthodox Christians ask forgiveness from each other. We've chosen a literal translation here instead of "Shrovetide." Shrovetide is the time of carnival before the beginning of Lent. Many thanks to Slava Yastremski for pointing this out.

9   Aleksandr Blok (1880-1921). The most famous of the Russian Symbolist poets and author of the long poem "The Twelve" about the Russian Revolution.

10   Blok's name with the hard sign at the end of the name was originally five letters long. With orthographic reforms after the Russian Revolution it became four letters long when the hard signs at the end of nouns was dropped.

11   Tsvetaeva's collection *The Swan's Encampment* consisted of poems about the Russian Civil War between the Bolshevik Red Army and the White Army, which lasted from 1917-1922. Tsvetaeva's husband Sergei Efron served on the side of the White Army in southern Russia while Tsvetaeva remained in Moscow with their children Ariadna

and Irina. At the end of the war Efron was evacuated from the Crimea, and he and Tsvetaeva were reunited in emigration in Prague in 1922.

12   Andre Chenier was a French poet, who was a precursor of the Romantic movement. He was executed during the French Revolution allegedly for "crimes against the state." Tsvetaeva is unmistakably associating herself with the French poet. He was taken from the La Conciergerie prison in Paris to his execution on July 25, 1794.

13   A reference to the image in the Revelation of St. John the Divine 12:3, 12:7-9.

14   A reference to the representation of Paradise/The Garden of Eden as a white circle that includes images of trees on it in Russian icons, such as the icon "O Thee Rejoiceth." For visual examples of it, see: http://www.vidania.ru/icony/icon_o_tebe_raduetsya.html.

15   The epigraph comes from Fedor Tiutchev's famous poem of 1820—"Videnie" (A Vision); "There is a certain hour, in the night, of universal silence (Est' nekii chas, v nochi, vsemirnogo molchan'ia)."

16   Literally a bed sheet. In Tsvetaeva's poetics, the sheet is an emblem of physicality, which leads to death and destruction. The poet instead seeks salvation in the spiritual. Thus for Tsvetaeva the image suggests a "winding sheet."

17   The Jordan has numerous Biblical associations. Firstly, it represents the eastern border of the Promised Land, the river that Joshua crossed with the Israelites. Also in the Old Testament in the Book of Kings (II: 5) it marks the place where Naaman the Syrian was directed to wash seven times to cure his leprosy. In the New Testament, John the Baptist baptizes Christ in the Jordan. In the Russian

tradition, Jordan also means the hole in the ice on a river made during the January Holiday of Theophany, from which water is taken to symbolically cleanse Orthodox Christians of their sins and to bless their houses.

18 The cycle is dedicated to Tsvetaeva's close Czech friend Anna Antonovna Teskova (1872-1954), whom she befriended in Prague in 1924. After moving to Paris, Tsvetaeva continued a lengthy correspondence with Teskova until Tsvetaeva's return to the Soviet Union in 1939.

19 Tsvetaeva was herself prematurely gray, a fact that she considered to be a sign of her mature and highly developed inner spirit. Especially see her poem "Gray Hair" (Sedye volosy) for her poetic meditation on this topic. She curiously left that poem out of her collection *After Russia* even though it was written in the same time period.

20 Or: "inflamed" or "burning" blood.

21 The cycle began as a reaction to Boris Pasternak's impending return to Russia from Berlin on March 18, 1923.

22 An inexact quote from Johann Christian Hölderlin's (1770-1843) *Hyperion*. The translation from the German is as follows: "The billow of the heart would not froth up so beautifully and would become spirit, if the old silent rock, fate, did not stand against it." My gratitude to Marcia Morris for assisting me with the translation of this passage.

23 Among the ancients, the highest heaven, a region where pure light and fire exist.

24 "Sryv" can also be translated as "failure."

25 "Prostite" can also be translated as "forgive."

26 In Greek mythology, Ariadne, the daughter of King Minos, falls in love with the Athenian Theseus and helps him escape from the Minotaur in the labyrinth on Crete. She gives him a ball of twine,

which he unravels as he enters the labyrinth. Theseus slays the Minotaur, escapes the labyrinth, and sails away with Ariadne and his crew. He leaves her on the isle of Naxos to recover from her seasickness and a storm sweeps the ship away. Ariadne lies dead on the shore when Theseus returns with his crew. The god Dionysus, enthralled by the beauty of the dead Ariadne, takes her for his immortal wife. In the Gustav Schwab version of the myth—which Tsvetaeva certainly used as her source—Dionysus appears to Theseus in a dream, in which he declares Ariadne to be his bride. In order not to bring down the wrath of the god, Theseus complies and gives up his bride.

27   (1895?-1930). A childhood friend of Tsvetaeva's and the sister of Yuri Zavadsky, an actor in the Third Studio of MKhAT. Tsvetaeva later met her again in the emigration in Paris. In depictions of her, Tsvetaeva concentrates on describing her pale beauty and her infirmity, the latter of which resulted in a premature death.

28   Or: a griffin.

29   A reference to the legendary inscription on Solomon's seal.

30   This poem coincides with the end of Tsvetaeva's unhappy love affair with Konstantin Rodzevich in mid-to-late September 1923. The long poems "Poem of the Mountain" and "Poem of the End" chronicle her relationship with him. Her depressed emotional state led her back to walk to her favorite Prague sights for her meditations, particularly to the statue of the Knight Bruncvik at the Charles Bridge overlooking the Vltava River in Prague. A picture of the statue can be found online here: http://www.kralovskacesta.cz/en/tour/objects/statue-of-bruncvik.html.

31   We have opted to translate Tsvetaeva's neologism created by the dash in the middle of the word "mosto—viny," which literally means "bridge planks" without the dash, but in this instance suggests a bridge of guilt or the guilt of the bridge.

32   The addressee of the poem is Mark Slonim (1894-1976), a literary critic and editor of the Prague émigré journal *The Will of Russia* (*Volia Rossii*), in which Tsvetaeva often published.

33   Zeus is depicted in Plato's *Phaedrus* as holding the reins of a winged chariot. His steeds were born of the four winds.

34   An Italian town renowned for its marble and for its academy of sculpture.

35   The mythical first wife of Adam and the mother of evil spirits according to Talmudic legend.

36   Literally a person from Shulem. The Shulamite is the object of King Solomon's affection and the heroine of the Song of Songs.

37   A reference to Alexander Borodin's opera *Prince Igor*, based on the famous epic *The Lay of Igor's Campaign* (*Slovo o polku Igoreve*). The choreographer Mikhail Fokin included the Polovtsian Dances in the first season of Sergei Diaghilev's Ballet Russe in Paris that quickly became a sensation for its energy and non-classical approach to ballet.

38   A reference to Alexander Pushkin's long poem "The Gypsies" ("Tsygany"; 1824).

39   A reference to Alexander Pushkin's poem "Song of Oleg's Prophecy" ("Pesn' o veshchem Olege"; 1822), in which the legendary Prince Oleg, who defeated the Greeks at Constantinople (Tsargrad, as it was known to the Russians in Oleg's time), was told a prophecy that he would die because

of his horse. Oleg exiled the horse, but after the horse died, went to visit his remains. When he placed his foot on the skull of his horse, a snake came out of it and killed him with its venom.

40   Literally "bogatyr" here, the superheroes of Russian folktales and legends such as Ilya Muromets and Alyosha Popovich.

41   A possible reference to the revolutionary ballet by Igor Stravinsky, *The Rite of Spring* (1913), performed during the second season of Diaghilev's Ballet Russe, in which the dancing is accompanied by shouts of the dancers – " Ah, Oh, Eh."

42   Tsvetaeva has indicated that this poem is addressed to Boris Pasternak. In the poem she plays extensively on the Russian prefix "raz-", meaning "to divide" or "to scatter in many directions."

43   Tsvetaeva likely has in mind the Orthodox marriage ceremony, during which the choir sings the liturgical chant of *alleluia* (praise to the Lord), as well as in the Divine Liturgy.

44   The art of (sexual) love in Latin.

45   The 23-poem cycle is dedicated to the actor Yuri Zavadsky (1894-1977).

46   The famous Italian goldsmith Benvenuto Cellini (1500-1571).

47   From the "Poems for Pushkin" cycle.

48   A reference to Tsar Nicholas I, who appointed himself Alexander Pushkin's censor and persecuted him. It is generally believed that he was responsible for Pushkin's death in a duel in 1837.

49   A reference to the suppression of the so-called November or Cadet Uprising of 1830-1831, which was eventually harshly subdued by superior Russian Imperial forces.

50   From Hölderlin's *Hyperion*. The translation would be: O, my love! Does this speech surprise you? Everyone who parts speaks as though they are drunk and loves solemnity.

51   "Mir," translated as "world" here, could also be translated as "peace."

52   According to the Greek myth, Persephone was abducted by Hades, who tricked her into eating pomegranate seeds, the food of the underworld, and because of that she had to spend the winter months there. Homer describes her as the formidable, venerable majestic queen of the underworld, who carries into effect the curses of men upon the souls of the dead.

53   A reference to Revelations 22: 12.

54   Hagar was Abraham's wife Sarah's slave. Sarah gave her to Abraham to bear children, and Hagar gave birth to Ishmael. Then Sarah, fearing that Ishmael could be competition for her son Isaac, wanted to eliminate him. God told Abraham to give Hagar and her son freedom, which Abraham did, sending them away into the desert. A well that appeared miraculously saved their lives.

55   The Latin *mori* (from the expression *memento mori*, meaning, remember that you will die) sounds in Russian just like "more" (the sea), which is what Tsvetaeva writes in the original.

56   A reference to the famous Bear Moat in the Czech Krumlow Castle that goes back to the 17th century when it was built as a means of protection and then became one of the main attractions of Southern Czechia.

57   I.e., Instead of that stone (mountains on me) there will be a flat one (a gravestone). [Tsvetaeva's note]

58   It is considered good luck in the Eastern Slavic tradition to have a stork build a nest on your roof.

59   That is, "Thou Shalt Not Commit Adultery."
60   A quote from the spiritual verses "The Lament of Joseph the Beautiful upon Being Sold by His Brothers into Slavery in Egypt" based on Genesis 37.
61   A reference to one of the wonders of the world – the Hanging Gardens of Babylon, created by the legendary Assyrian Queen Semiramis.
62   Possibly a reference to the blind bard Homer.
63   A possible reference to the river Vltava running through Prague. The Vltava was a symbol of the river Lethe for Tsvetaeva. (See: http://www.ruskerealie.zcu.cz/texts/text2-12-11.php).
64   Tsvetaeva is playing on the saying "u nego ryl'tse v pushku" (literally: he has down all over his snout, that is, face in the trough (i.e., the guilt is evident). Special thanks to Slava Yastremski for pointing this out.
65   Berthold Schwartz is considered to have been the inventor of gunpowder.
66   The character from the 18th century epistolary novel *Clarissa* (1748) by Samuel Richardson. In the novel Lovelace seduces the 16-year old Clarissa. In the Russian cultural tradition Lovelace's name became synonymous with profligate men.
67   This is an exact quote from the Song of Songs 8:6. In the Russian Bible it is: "kak pechat', na serdtse tvoe, kak persten' na ruku tvoiu."
68   A reference to Cleopatra, who dissolved a precious black pearl in a glass of wine to impress Mark Antony.
69   Holkonda is a mountain in India famous for its diamond mines.
70   Tsvetaeva is referring to Rembrandt's famous painting "Danaë," which is located in the Hermitage Museum

in St. Petersburg, in which Zeus comes to the naked Danaë as a shower of gold.

71   A reference to King Solomon in Tarot fortune telling where he is associated with astrological signs of the planets. The pentacles of all the planets should be made on Mercury day (Wednesday) and Mercury hour, with the Moon in an air or earth sign, as well as waxing, and on an even day after the New Moon. *Greater Key of Solomon & the Pentacles of Solomon*.

72   This can also be read as "Wow! Yes to that!"

73   The first part of "den' – ga" (den') separately means "day." So the line can also have the echoed reading of "A day for death."

74   Tsvetaeva's realized metaphor is untranslatable. In the original "Ras—staemsia" has four syllables and paronomastically breaks down into the components "raz" (meaning "one") and the second syllable "sta" ("one hundred" in the genitive case meaning "of a hundred").

75   A reference to the Russian Cubo-Futurist poet Velimir Khlebnikov, who was the most innovative and daring of all Russian Futurists. He claimed to be an inventor of "trans-rational language," that is, a language whose meaning lies in the linguistic meaning of the phonetic components of words. In particular the reference to the swan is attributed to Khlebnikov's longer poem "Lightworld" (Svetomir), in which we see white, black and red swans crying for the world.

76   Literally two-pood soles. A pood is a Russian measurement roughly weighing 36 pounds.

77   Tsvetaeva had great empathy for the Jewish people for their being persecuted. The fact that her husband Sergei Efron came from a Jewish family caused her stern Orthodox Christian father considerable consternation. Tsvetaeva's

empathy always stood with the downtrodden. See especially her poem "To the Jewish People" (1916), in which she writes that "all poets are Jews."

78   A reference to Tsvetaeva's Polish origins and to the character of the Polish woman Marina Mnishek, who became first a concubine and then the wife of the False Dimitry (the supposedly dead son of Ivan the Terrible, who fought Boris Godunov for the Russian throne).

79   A reference to Fyodor Dostoevsky's novel *Crime and Punishment*, in which the young man Raskolnikov kills an old woman pawnbroker in order to prove his idea that everything is permitted for him because he is an extraordinary man.

A note on the translators

Michael M. Naydan is Woskob Family Professor of Ukrainian Studies and Professor of Slavic Languages and Literatures at The Pennsylvania State University. He has edited, translated and co-translated 30 books from Russian and Ukrainian and has published over 30 articles and more than 50 translations in scholarly and literary journals. Most recently he edited and co-translated *Herstories: An Anthology of Contemporary Ukrainian Women Prose Writers* for Glagoslav Publishers in 2014. He previously co-translated Marina Tsvetaeva's collection *After Russia* with Slava Yastremski for Ardis Publishers in 1992.

Slava I. Yastremski is Professor of Russian literature at Bucknell University where he teaches Russian language and literature, theater and film studies, and courses in the comparative humanities. He has co-translated five books of translations of Russian authors with Michael Naydan including separate volumes of Olga Sedakova's poetry and prose with Bucknell University Press, a volume of Igor Klekh's prose *A Country the Size of Binoculars* with Northwestern University Press in 2004, and Nadezhda Ptushkina's plays for Glagoslav Publishers in 2013. He additionally has published translations with Joel Wilkinson of Vassily Aksyonov's short stories with Ardis Publishers in 1985 under the title *Surplussed Barrelware* and with Catharine Theimer Nepomnyashchy of Andrei Sinyavsky's *Strolls with Pushkin* with Yale University Press in 1993.

Tess Gallagher (born 1943) is a well-known American poet, short story writer, essayist, and translator. Of her twelve books of published poetry, *Midnight Lantern: New and Selected Poems* (Graywolf Press, 2011) is her latest. Additionally she has published three books of short stories including *The Man From Kinvara: Selected Stories* (Graywolf Press, 2009) and two collections of essays with University of Michigan Press. A winner of a Gugenheim Foundation fellowship and two National Endowment for the Arts awards, she has taught widely at various American universities even after her retirement from the faculty of Syracuse University. In her work as a co-translator she has published a number of Liliana Ursu's poems from Romanian. She has also been a staunch promoter of her husband Ray Carver's literary legacy, most recently having given permission to use Ray Carver's writings as the basis for the highly successful award-winning movie *Birdman*.

Dear Reader,

Thank you for purchasing this book.

We at Glagoslav Publications are glad to welcome you, and hope that you find our books a source of knowledge and inspiration.

We want to show the beauty and depth of the Slavic region to everyone looking to expand their horizons and learn something new about different cultures, different people, and we believe that with this book we have managed to do just that.

Now that you've got to know us, we want to get to know you. We value communication with our readers and want to hear from you!

We offer several options:

- Join our Book Club on Goodreads, Library Thing and Shelfari, and receive special offers and information about our giveaways;
- Share your opinion about our books on Amazon, Barnes & Noble, Waterstones and other bookstores;
- Join us on Facebook and Twitter for updates on our publications and news about our authors;
- Visit our site www.glagoslav.com to check out our Catalogue and subscribe to our Newsletter.

Glagoslav Publications is getting ready to release a new collection and planning some interesting surprises — stay with us to find out!

Glagoslav Publications
Office 36, 88-90 Hatton Garden
EC1N 8PN London, UK
Tel: + 44 (0) 20 32 86 99 82
Email: contact@glagoslav.com

Glagoslav Publications Catalogue

- *The Time of Women* by Elena Chizhova
- *Sin* by Zakhar Prilepin
- *Hardly Ever Otherwise* by Maria Matios
- *The Lost Button* by Irene Rozdobudko
- *Khatyn* by Ales Adamovich
- *Christened with Crosses* by Eduard Kochergin
- *The Vital Needs of the Dead* by Igor Sakhnovsky
- *A Poet and Bin Laden* by Hamid Ismailov
- *Kobzar* by Taras Shevchenko
- *White Shanghai* by Elvira Baryakina
- *The Stone Bridge* by Alexander Terekhov
- *King Stakh's Wild Hunt* by Uladzimir Karatkevich
- *Depeche Mode* by Serhii Zhadan
- *Saraband Sarah's Band* by Larysa Denysenko
- *Herstories*, An Anthology of New Ukrainian Women Prose Writers
- *The Hawks of Peace* by Dmitry Rogozin
  by Leonid Andreev
- *The Battle of the Sexes Russian Style* by Nadezhda Ptushkina
- *A Book Without Photographs* by Sergey Shargunov
- *Sankya* by Zakhar Prilepin
- *Wolf Messing - The True Story of Russia's Greatest Psychic* by Tatiana Lungin
- *Good Stalin* by Victor Erofeyev
- *Solar Plexus* by Rustam Ibragimbekov
- *Don't Call me a Victim!* by Dina Yafasova
- *A History of Belarus* by Lubov Bazan
- *Children's Fashion of the Russian Empire* by Alexander Vasiliev
- *Empire of Corruption - The Russian National Pastime* by Vladimir Soloviev
- *Heroes of the 90s - People and Money. The Modern History of Russian Capitalism*
- *Boris Yeltsin - The Decade that Shook the World* by Boris Minaev
- *A Man Of Change - A study of the political life of Boris Yeltsin*
- *Gnedich* by Maria Rybakova

More coming soon...

www.ingramcontent.com/pod-product-compliance
Lightning Source LLC
Chambersburg PA
CBHW020908080526
44589CB00011B/495